STAR CHEFS
on the road

10 CULINARY MASTERS SHARE STORIES AND RECIPES

American Express Publishing Corporation
1120 Avenue of the Americas, New York, NY 10036

© 2005 American Express Publishing Corporation

For more information on FOOD & WINE Books,
go to foodandwine.com/fwbooks or call 800-284-4145.

Assouline Publishing
601 West 26th Street, 18th Floor
New York, NY 10001 USA
Tel: 212-989-6810 Fax: 212-647-0005
www.assouline.com

FOOD&WINE

STAR CHEFS
on the road

10 CULINARY MASTERS SHARE STORIES AND RECIPES

For more information on FOOD & WINE Books,
log on to foodandwine.com/fwbooks or call 800-284-4145.

Assouline Publishing
601 West 26th Street, 18th Floor
New York, NY 10001 USA
Tel: 212-989-6810 Fax: 212-647-0005
www.assouline.com

ISBN: 1-932624-07-4
Color separation: Studio L.P.T. (United States)
Printed by Toppan (China)

As the Editor in Chief of FOOD & WINE, I'm always on the lookout for new experiences—a "what's next" junkie. But if I went to every single place on the planet that intrigued me, I'd never spend a day in the office. Not going to happen. So I rely on the magazine's tireless scouts, passionate explorers who travel the world and then bring it back to me. In the quest for unusual flavors and places, I often turn to chefs. Think about it: They need to keep their culinary repertoire fresh and their minds engaged beyond the kitchen, so they head out of town—sometimes even back to their hometowns. Hearing about their adventures, I feel as if I've had a new experience myself.

Some of my favorite pieces ever published in F&W are collected in this book. Jacques Pépin, the extraordinary cooking teacher, traveled to Botswana and Zambia; I was fascinated to hear how much he learned from the local cooks and Bushmen he met there. He even got used to eating the crunchy, nutty, buttery snack better known as harvester termites. I think I'll stick with the chicken and peanut stew the trip inspired him to create when he came back home. I'll always remember talking to Eric Ripert right after he returned from a trip to Puerto Rico. He promised that I'd see the visit's influence on the cuisine at his exquisite four-star New York City restaurant, Le Bernardin. He also swore that he'd finally learned to dance to salsa music. During our conversation about his trip to Shanghai, Jean-Georges Vongerichten almost convinced me to go there myself. He was so excited about the markets, the food stalls and, of course, the opening of his 15th restaurant, Jean Georges Shanghai. China is where it's all happening now, he said.

Each chef has a wonderful story to tell, and I'm delighted to share them all with you. Whether you're a dreamer or a doer, I think you'll find them exciting.

Dana Cowin
Editor in Chief
FOOD & WINE

JACQUES PÉPIN
Botswana & Zambia

On a luxurious African wilderness trip, TV chef Jacques Pépin stays at Tongabezi in Zambia, ABOVE, and, in Botswana, at San Camp, OPPOSITE, owned by Ralph Bousfield and Catherine Raphaely.

We call these Desert Pringles," Ralph Bousfield says, wielding a handful of salt grass. "Try one!" Jacques Pépin breaks off a spiky blade, tastes and frowns. Though spring hares crave it, salt grass turns out to be a less satisfying snack than the next item on the menu, harvester termites. "They're crunchy," Pépin says, chewing one. "Quite nutty, buttery." Pépin is sampling bush food at Bousfield's San Camp, an outpost in the Kalahari Desert. It's the first stop on a seven-night safari that will take us through the southern part of Africa, from Botswana to Zambia. Of course, seven years would be a more realistic time frame for exploring this vast terrain, but Pépin has a lot on his plate, with two TV series and his duties as a dean of the French Culinary Institute in New York City. On this tour, he is going to get a concentrated taste of the continent, even if it only serves to whet his appetite for a return visit. Africa does this. Nobody can shrug off the huge plains and rivers and skies, the wild beasts, the music and the people, even the shameful, beautiful remnants of colonialism. Nobody who has been here once is immune from wishing to come back. African food, varied as it is, is not normally the draw. Too often, for the safari visitor at least, menus promise that dreaded noncuisine

Pépin's Chicken and Peanut Stew. OPPOSITE:
Tongabezi Lodge, overlooking the Zambezi.

known as "international"—partly a legacy of the colonial era, partly the product of lowest-common-denominator tourism economics. The two camps on Pépin's itinerary, however, are way more sophisticated than that. Here at San Camp, the chefs conjure up wonderful food in the middle of the desert; at Tongabezi, the resort in Zambia where we will spend three days at the end of the week, the chefs are skilled at incorporating African ingredients into Western dishes. From working with the cooks in these places, Pépin is hoping to discover something of southern African food, both in its undiluted state and as it has been adapted for travelers. The Kalahari itself is all about adaptation. Every living thing here has developed ingenious ways to survive, from the salt grass, which would pickle itself alive if it hadn't learned to pump salt out through its leaves, to the Sua Kwe Bushmen, who have figured out how to subsist on and around the Makgadikgadi salt pans, an astonishing expanse that was once a vast saltwater lake roughly the size of Switzerland. The land appears barren of life, but the more we look, the more we see. Every few yards our handsome and logorrheic guide, biologist Chris Varco, whips out his binoculars. "Look! Impalas! That's so rare here. They're obviously on a day trip." (Little do they know they're on tonight's menu. Africa is harsh.) "See there! A secretary bird eating a snake. Those birds hate to fly. They hunt on foot." We see helicopter birds taking off vertically, and ostriches striding like Nureyev, and *mopane* trees folding their leaves like butterfly wings in the sun.

fter our introduction to the Kalahari, we head back to San Camp. The most amazing desert adaptation of all may be the one performed here by Bousfield and his wife, Catherine Raphaely, who have created a fantastical outpost—with canvas tents, hardwood floors, Persian carpets, leather trunks and antiques—out of the only positive aspect of colonialism, its visual style. Each day a very basic kitchen produces three-course feasts, complete with fresh-baked breads, from a single weekly delivery of provisions. The men who accomplish this feat are Benson Mwenda, the head chef, and his sous-chef, Foster Bube. Raphaely, who taught them most of what they know about Western cooking, is keen for the two (plus the chefs from San's sister camp, Jack's) to spend time with Pépin. "By meeting you," she explains to him, "they'll see that being a chef is an international profession and a man's profession. I don't want them to think it's a white madam's thing."

Perhaps because they have been told of Pépin's exalted status, or perhaps because the white madam is hovering, Mwenda and Bube are a little shy at first. Pépin quickly breaks the ice with some sleight of hand from his apprentice days, creating butter roses and caramel cages, incongruous froufrou that the other chefs find hilarious and pick up instantly. In no time, the language of food has created a bond among the three men. For the remainder of his stay at San, Pépin is forever disappearing, only to be discovered rummaging in the freezer with Mwenda.

The truth is, Pépin is just as eager to learn from Mwenda and Bube as they are to learn from him. He wants to know about the privations and challenges of cooking in the bush,

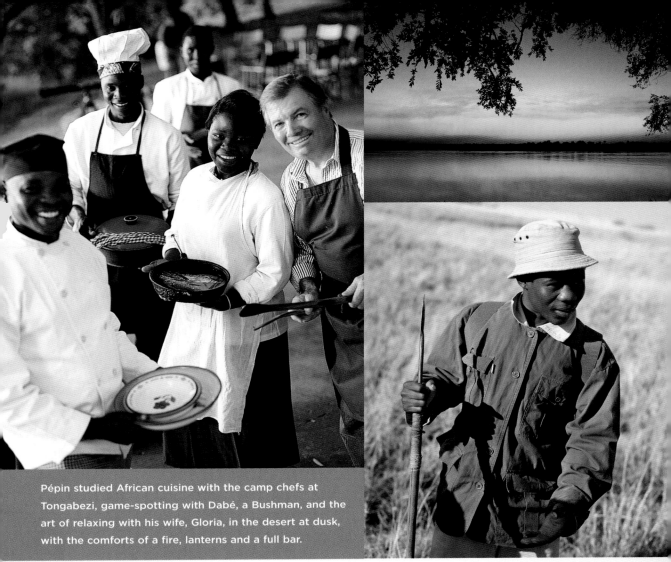

Pépin studied African cuisine with the camp chefs at
Tongabezi, game-spotting with Dabé, a Bushman, and the
art of relaxing with his wife, Gloria, in the desert at dusk,
with the comforts of a fire, lanterns and a full bar.

A visit to the Livingstone Market in Zambia inspired Pépin's Peanut-Crusted Trout, OPPOSITE.

where opportunism in the use of ingredients is key, and he is even more interested in the real cuisine of the land, the dishes Mwenda's and Bube's mothers taught them. But this will have to wait for a special delivery of bush ingredients. So their first joint venture becomes a Franco-African dinner menu. They select impala, which Pépin proceeds to rub with rosemary and lemon zest. "Don't use the lemon juice," he explains to Mwenda and Bube. "The acid will cook the meat." For dessert, the chefs infuse milk with *rooibos* tea (which takes the place of coffee in half the continent) for a crème anglaise.

At dusk, before the actual cooking, we head out once more into the desert on special motorbikes with four fat tires. We chase the twilight deep into the Makgadikgadi, then park and recline on the salt plain to watch the night sky. This is the proverbial middle of nowhere, nothing but salt and stars, atmosphere and silence, from horizon to horizon. It's a place that shifts your axis forever. Pépin dips a finger into the salt and pops it in his mouth. "Just like *fleur de sel,*" he declares—the world's most expensive salt.

With difficulty we tear ourselves away to ride home. En route, we spot a fire up ahead. "Be careful," Varco says. "It's poachers. They could be armed." But in the best surprise the desert has yet yielded, the "poachers" turn out to be Mwenda and Bube, who are preparing a plum sauce and baking sweet potato gratins in a Dutch oven on the campfire. A huge table has been set for dinner and a full bar has miraculously appeared right on the salt flats. Pépin picks up a pan and joins the chefs as they sear the impala.

"Out here," he laughs, "I don't feel like a cook, I feel like a shaman."

The following day, when the bush ingredients arrive, Mwenda and Bube set to work teaching the teacher about their food. There are jars of *marula* fruit jam and sacks of *mielepap* meal, a ground maize very like polenta. There are dried melons; *morogo* (also known as wild spinach); dried *mopane* worms; and *buyu,* the fruit of the baobab tree, which yields the original version of cream of tartar. "It's sensational," Pépin says, chewing a piece of *buyu,* "powdery, white and tart."

"What do you do with dried melon?" he asks Mwenda.

"You can boil the melon for about three hours and eat it with sugar; and you can drink

the liquid separately as a soup alongside *mielepap* meal."

"When would you eat that?" he asks. "For breakfast?"

"Yes, like a soft porridge, or else for dinner with relishes."

"What relishes?"

"*Mopane* worms, or *seswaa,* or *morogo.*"

"What is *seswaa*? How do you prepare the *morogo*?"

Soon, Mwenda and Bube start answering Pépin's questions by preparing a meal, which they'll take out into the desert and sample at sunset. *Seswaa* is an economical long-cooked meat stew; the *mopane* worms and the *morogo* are rehydrated and cooked with onions and tomatoes.

The next morning, Pépin says his good-byes to Mwenda and Bube and we set out for Zambia. At Victoria Falls on the border we meet up with Cherri Briggs, president of Explore, the custom safari outfit that designed our trip. Briggs knows every corner of Africa. Zambia, she thinks, is the most beautiful, unspoiled country on the continent; along the road to Tongabezi, it certainly looks green and promising. If the desert was about adaptation, Tongabezi, a cross between a Caribbean resort and the Swiss Family Robinson's tree house, is about relaxation. My room is shaped like an amphitheater, with one huge curved wall painted with murals and the Zambezi River where the audience should be. The bed could comfortably sleep six. Beneath my mosquito netting, I fall asleep to a hippo lullaby. Pépin is clearly relieved that the kitchen at Tongabezi is professional, if a little eccentric, with battered aluminum pans where the All-Clad should be. One reason things are in good order here is the influence of the camp's Scottish chef, Craig Higgins. We were looking forward to meeting him, but there is some disappointing news. He tried to hang on for Pépin, we are told, through a nasty case of malaria, only to succumb to a burst appendix. He has flown home to Scotland to recover. But we are in the capable hands of his African protégés, with George Kalaluka at the helm and his sous-chefs, Zui, Rogers, Agnes and Albert, assisting him. They have inherited Higgins's inventive African-accented recipes: butternut and cassava leaf ravioli with sun-dried tomatoes; fritters of *kapenta,* the Zambian version of whitebait; crocodile marinated in yogurt; and guava torte.

After touring the kitchen, we all head to Livingstone Market where Kalaluka, a father of three, shops for his family. He and Pépin hit it off famously, poring over dried fish and live fowl, greens and oils and Kalahari salt. Pépin examines every fish, leaf, root and fruit; for him, this market is better than any museum. In close consultation with Kalaluka, he picks the freshest greens, some of the tiny eggplants called *impua,* cabbages and tomatoes. Pépin attracts a giggling crowd of shoppers—we are the only tourists here—especially when he makes a comedy act out of learning to pound groundnuts with a big stick. He also encourages Kalaluka to pose with a large and irritable chicken. "You know, when we were kids we'd kill the chicken by cutting under the tongue, and we'd keep the blood for

After watching the night sky over the Makgadikgadi salt flats, Pépin meets with Benson Mwenda and Foster Bube to tend to the campfire and talk of Franco-African inventions.

"Out here, I don't feel like a cook, I feel like a shaman."

JACQUES PÉPIN

The Kalahari Desert around San Camp may seem barren, but it is actually full of life.

the sauce," Pépin says. Kalaluka explains that at Tongabezi, they buy their chickens already dead. We taste a carton of Shake Shake 7 Days, a millet beer fermented for six days and drunk on the seventh. (Do not try this.) Finally, we repair to the nearby Mosi-oi-tunya Game Park to view, at last, some really big animals.

We start with warthogs (Pépin is fond of them, having made warthog prosciutto on a trip to Senegal a couple of years ago). Then come crowds of malevolent jack-hammer baboons and herds of bouncing impalas and placid zebras. A pair of giraffes appear, elegant in slow motion, and, finally, the biggest thrill of all: elephants. "This is the way to see game," Briggs says. "Animals in the zoo are like human beings in a mental hospital."

Time at Tongabezi, filled with eating, lazing, game watching and (for the brave) white-water rafting, passes at cheetah speed. All too soon, it is time to make our way to Tongabezi's tiny downriver island outpost, Sindabezi, for our farewell lunch. We reach it by canoe. Never get between a hippo and the shore, Briggs warns. They hate that. Despite their Beanie Baby looks and vegetarian diet, these creatures are the biggest killers of humans in Africa, more dangerous even than crocodiles. The lower Zambezi teems with both. We row very, very carefully. At Sindabezi, Pépin enjoys a meal cooked entirely by Kalaluka, a simple salad of the youngest leaves (a rare commodity) and herbs from the Tongabezi garden, freshly baked rolls and spiced, marinated, wood-fired beef fillet en brochette. Pépin is amused to hear that beef fillet is cheap and plentiful here and the meat at the bone is prized.

"George's food," Pépin confides, as if grading one of his students at the French Culinary Institute, "is well balanced and substantive. He has a really good, solid sense of seasoning. A natural." Thus proving what we knew all along, but have found afresh in Africa—as Pépin puts it: "You don't have to torture yourself to express yourself. You are within the food you make whether you like it or not."

BY KATE SEKULES

TRAVEL TIPS

FLYING TO AFRICA

• One of the best ways to get to southern Africa is to take VIRGIN ATLANTIC from New York City to Johannesburg via London, as Pépin did. ("The best transatlantic flight I've ever taken," he says.) Round-trip airfare begins at about $1,500 for Economy and $6,000 for Upper Class (800-862-8621). With so much going on in London these days, you might want to extend your stopover into a mini vacation.

EXPLORING AFRICA

• An outfit that's called EXPLORE (888-LYONESS or exploreafrica.net) customizes trips throughout the continent. An itinerary similar to Pépin's, with three nights each at San Camp (or its sister camp, Jack's) and Tongabezi, plus three nights at Chief's Camp in the Okavango Delta of Botswana, is $6,175, including transfers, charter flights, lodging (based on double occupancy) and meals, but not including international flights or commercial flights within Africa.

San Camp looks as if it could have been the base for an expedition in the 1930s or '40s.

At San Camp, Pépin collects wild russet bush willow leaves to steep in hot water.

Chicken and Peanut Stew

4 TO 6 SERVINGS

Jacques Pépin created this hearty stew with ingredients he found at the Livingstone Market. Peanuts are a South African staple and figure prominently in local dishes.

½ cup cornmeal

Salt and freshly ground pepper

One 3½-pound chicken, cut into
    8 pieces, rinsed and patted dry

¼ cup vegetable oil

2 small onions, coarsely chopped

1 jalapeño, seeded and minced

1 cup water

½ cup white wine vinegar

½ cup raw peanuts (2½ ounces)

8 unpeeled garlic cloves

1 large sweet potato, peeled and cut
    into 1½-inch chunks

1½ pounds long thin eggplants, sliced
    crosswise 1½ inches thick

2 small yellow squash, sliced
    crosswise 1½ inches thick

1 bunch scallions, cut into
    2-inch pieces

1. In a sturdy plastic bag, combine the cornmeal with salt and pepper. Add the chicken in batches and shake to coat.

2. In a large heavy casserole, heat the oil until shimmering. Add the chicken and fry over moderately high heat, turning once, until well-browned, about 12 minutes; reduce the heat if the chicken browns too quickly. Transfer the chicken to a large platter.

3. Pour off all but 2 tablespoons of the fat in the casserole. Add the onions and jalapeño and cook over low heat until just softened, about 3 minutes. Add the water, vinegar, peanuts and garlic, season with salt and pepper and bring to a simmer. Return the chicken to the casserole, cover and simmer over low heat until tender and cooked through, about 45 minutes. Transfer the chicken to a platter.

4. Add the sweet potato, eggplants and yellow squash to the casserole. Cover and cook over low heat until the vegetables are very tender, 1 hour. Return the chicken to the casserole, add the scallions and simmer until the scallions are tender, 12 minutes. Season with salt and pepper and serve.

MAKE AHEAD The stew can be refrigerated overnight.

WINE This chicken stew pairs well with a medium-bodied, bright-flavored red, like a South African Pinotage.

Peanut-Crusted Fish with Swiss Chard

4 SERVINGS

The Swiss chard is a stand-in for the robust green sweet potato leaves Pépin discovered in Africa, and fresh trout replaces the Kalahari river bream he found there.

½ cup plus 3 tablespoons
    vegetable oil

4 garlic cloves, minced

⅓ cup toasted sunflower or
    pumpkin seeds

2 pounds Swiss chard, stems
    removed, leaves coarsely chopped

½ teaspoon Tabasco, plus more
    for serving

Salt and freshly ground pepper

1 large tomato, coarsely chopped

1 cup peanuts (5 ounces)

1 tablespoon cornmeal

Four 5-ounce trout fillets

1 large egg white, lightly beaten

Lemon wedges, for serving

1. In a large deep skillet, heat 3 tablespoons of the oil. Add the garlic and sunflower seeds and cook over moderate heat, stirring frequently, until golden, about 2 minutes. Add the chard leaves, a handful at a time, and

Pépin searches for wildlife, then returns to San Camp to make herbal tea.

cook until just wilted before adding more. Continue cooking over moderate heat until tender, about 5 minutes. Add the ½ teaspoon of Tabasco and season with salt and pepper. Add the tomato to the chard and remove from the heat; keep warm.

2. In a food processor, pulse the peanuts and cornmeal until finely ground. Spread the ground peanuts on a plate. Lightly brush the trout fillets with the egg white; season with salt. Dip the trout in the ground peanuts, pressing lightly to help the coating adhere.

3. In a skillet, heat the remaining ½ cup of oil until shimmering. Add the trout and fry over moderately high heat, turning once, until golden and crisp, about 3 minutes per side.

4. Mound the Swiss chard on a large platter or plates. Top with the fish and serve with Tabasco and lemon wedges.

WINE A crisp South African Sauvignon Blanc will go well with both the robust chard and the mild fish.

Rock Shandy

MAKES 1 DRINK

A holdover from colonial times, this refreshing drink is the sparkling cooler of choice at many African safari camps.

Ice

  2 tablespoons Rose's lime juice

  3 dashes Angostura bitters

Cold sparkling water

Fill half of a tall glass with ice. Add the Rose's lime juice and Angostura bitters and stir with a long-handled spoon. Fill the glass with sparkling water and serve.

Kalahari Venison Medallions with Plum Sauce

4 SERVINGS

Pépin developed this quick but sophisticated main dish using local African impala, but venison is a fine substitute.

  2 teaspoons finely grated lemon zest

  1 rosemary sprig, leaves removed

  2 tablespoons vegetable oil

Eight ½-inch-thick venison loin medallions (about 3 ounces each)

  2 tablespoons unsalted butter

Salt and freshly ground pepper

  ½ cup dry red wine

  1 cup beef or veal demiglace (see Note)

  2 tablespoons damson plum or seedless blackberry jam

1. In a small bowl, mix the lemon zest with the rosemary leaves and 1 tablespoon of the oil to form a paste. Coat the venison medallions with the paste and refrigerate for 2 hours.

2. In a large, heavy skillet, melt 1 teaspoon of the butter in the remaining 1 tablespoon of vegetable oil. Scrape the lemon and rosemary paste off the venison and season the medallions generously with salt and pepper. Add the meat to the pan and cook over high heat, turning once, until browned, 5 to 6 minutes. Transfer the venison medallions to a large plate, cover loosely with foil and keep warm.

3. Add the red wine to the skillet and bring to a boil over high heat, scraping up the browned bits from the bottom of the pan. Boil until a thick syrup forms, 4 to 5 minutes. Add the demiglace and boil until reduced to ½ cup, 8 to 10 minutes. Stir in the plum jam until melted, then add any accumulated juices from the meat. Swirl in the remaining 1 tablespoon plus 2 teaspoons of butter until blended. Drizzle the sauce over the meat and serve.

NOTE Beef and veal demiglace are available at specialty food shops..

PATRICIA QUINTANA
Mexico

OPPOSITE: Patricia Quintana, far left, gets guidance on how to make a traditional Yucatán dish from Reyna Gallegos, a local Mayan cook. ABOVE: Travelers to the Yucatán often visit the cathedral in Izamal, which was built on the ruins of a Mayan city.

t's early morning at the Mayan ruins of Uxmal on Mexico's Yucatán peninsula, and chef Patricia Quintana and I are the only people in sight. From our vantage point high on the steps of the crumbling Palacio del Gobernador, we see massive gray stone structures with fantastically carved serpents and masks all around us. There is nothing that an ancient Mayan wouldn't have recognized—except for us, that is. "You see," says Quintana as we make our way down the steep, uneven stones, "before the tour buses arrive, you can almost feel what it would have been like for the Mayans before the conquistadors." Quintana, the chef and co-owner of Izote, one of the hottest restaurants in Mexico City, is passionate about tracing Mexican cuisine back to its pre-Columbian roots. She's especially fascinated by the Yucatán, where she's made dozens of trips over the past quarter century to research her more than 14 cookbooks. Yucatán cuisine is distinctive partly because the region was geographically isolated from the rest of the country for centuries, Quintana explains as we head toward the market in the capital of Mérida, on the northwestern side of the peninsula. Our driver speeds along the Paseo de Montejo—a broad avenue lined with faded colonial mansions in varying states of restoration. This part of Mérida, just outside the center of the city, is architecturally

Chiles, citrus and tropical fruit like papayas figure prominently in Mexican cuisine.

reminiscent of Havana: The Yucatán peninsula juts into the Caribbean Sea, so Mérida is actually closer to Cuba than it is to Mexico City.

The Spanish influences on the cuisine are strong—the conquistadors arrived in the 16th century—but so are those of the Mayans, whom the Spanish were never quite able to obliterate, despite their bloody efforts. Northern Europeans have left their legacy too, particularly the Dutch: Holland was an active trading partner in the 19th century, when Mérida was the center for the production of henequen, a fiber traditionally used for making rope.

"The corn, the chocolate and the honey, the venison and wild turkey, squash, cucumbers, chiles and tomatoes are from the Mayans," Quintana says. "The pork and Seville oranges come from Spain, and the Edam cheese from the Dutch."

Edam? It sounds strange, but as we enter the dim, narrow lanes of the huge covered market, I see balls of Edam and Gouda everywhere, piled into pyramids next to dozens of bins of earth-toned *recados,* the ubiquitous herb-and-spice pastes. Quintana stops in front of the tubs of *recados.* "Each one of these is for a different dish, and people buy a few cents' worth to use that day," she says.

I lean over to catch a whiff of a ruddy paste made of annatto and other spices. The musky scent, sharp and very intense, is completely different from the nutty, grassy odor of the greenish one next to it, made of pumpkin seeds, or the peppery aroma of the brown paste behind it. "The dark one is a spice paste made of cloves, black peppercorns and other spices and tastes of earth and fruit," Quintana explains, raising three manicured fingers to her lips as if she were tasting it. "It's for *pavo en escabeche*—spice-rubbed turkey. There's a touch of vinegar in the sauce and a lot of onions and garlic. When I make it, I serve it with a roasted green-chile sauce and warm, soft tortillas."

This passion for cooking developed at an early age. The daughter of cattle ranchers, Quintana grew up in Mexico City and spent summers in Veracruz running barefoot through the houses of the workers, who would always give her a little treat—a sliver of pork, a nibble of tortilla, a ripe piece of fruit.

"I wanted to be like them," she confides. "I couldn't, of course, but I could learn their recipes, which define the essence of a person." So, with every gift of food, she began asking, "How do you make this?" And she would stay and watch the women cook every morning, moving from one house to the next to learn something new.

Watching Quintana maneuver quickly from stall to stall in the market, it's easy to imagine her as a little girl, inquisitive and earnest. Even as an adult, her efforts are rewarded with morsels of food. By asking an older Mayan woman wearing a *hipil* (a traditional white embroidered dress) about her roasting method, she talks her way into tastes of *cochinita pibil,* the pit-roasted pig marinated in sour Seville orange juice, garlic and that intense-smelling red *recado* made from annatto seeds.

"Before the Spanish introduced pigs," Quintana says as we eat the tender shreds of

Tortilla strips garnish a soothing, fragrant chicken and lime soup.

pork with pink pickled onions, "the Mayans pit-roasted venison with a similar *recado*. At Izote, I sometimes use the same paste for ribs."

This snack whets our appetite, but it's only 11:30, too early for lunch. So instead we head back to the Paseo de Montejo, and go to Dulcería y Sorbetería Colón, a sorbet shop and café where hordes of schoolchildren usually congregate in the afternoon. We pick five flavors of sorbet—including *nance* (similar to a yellow plum), *saramullo* (a tropical fruit that tastes like honeydew) and a fantastic sweet corn—and the house specialty, *merengue,* puffy pyramids that are soft inside but have crunchy brown tops. We also share a few rich, nut-colored shortbread cookies called *polvorones,* which are made with toasted flour and brown butter.

Afterward, we walk around the 16th-century Plaza Grande, Mérida's central square, where visitors come to see the colonial Spanish cathedral, the Casa de Montejo (a faded stately mansion converted to a bank) and a museum of contemporary Yucatán art. Snaking our way through the alleys behind the plaza, we end up at La Prosperidad, which specializes in *botanas* (little snacks), with a thatched roof and a band playing the greatest hits of Mexican pop. Occasionally, a diner gets up and sings, swaying arm in arm with the bandleader, a jeans-clad crooner in a Panama hat. Quintana orders us a round of *micheladas,* a tangy mix of lime juice, Worcestershire sauce, Tabasco and good, dark Yucatán beer. "It will bring your appetite back," she promises me.

A good thing, since the *botanas* that come out are irresistible; they include *papadzules,* hard-cooked eggs wrapped in corn tortillas with pumpkin-seed sauce and *sopa de lima,* a chicken-tortilla soup that's flavored with a fragrant local variety of sour lime. We eat all of it with *xnipek,* the ubiquitous table sauce of habanero chiles, scallions, citrus juices and cilantro. *Xnipek* translates to "dog's nose"—it's so spicy, one's nose starts to run after eating it.

By the time we leave La Prosperidad, it's started to rain, so we decide to head back to our hotel, the Hacienda Xcanatún, about 20 minutes outside the city. After drying off in my room, I meet Quintana at the hacienda's bar and order the house cocktail, an icy margarita-like concoction made with the local anise-and-honey liqueur called *xtabentún*. A few minutes later, Cristina Baker joins us. Baker and her husband, Jorge Ruz, bought the 18th-century hacienda 10 years ago and spent five years restoring the property, creating 18 suites, each with its own terrace, while keeping much of the traditional stone buildings intact. (In Mayan, *xcanatún* means "tall stone house.") Once part of a henequen-producing estate, the hacienda was abandoned in the 1950s or '60s after the introduction of synthetics for ropemaking reduced the demand for henequen. Many such estates throughout the Yucatán have been bought by young entrepreneurs and turned into small hotels and restaurants.

As we discuss our plans for the next day, Quintana says she must try the *queso relleno,* a stuffed cheese rind that's a Yucatán delicacy. "*Queso relleno* is really the

Cristina Baker and her husband, Jorge Ruz, BELOW, created Hacienda Xcanatún, a boutique hotel in a converted 18th-century hacienda about 20 minutes outside Mérida. The property includes 18 suites, each with its own terrace. Guests often visit the nearby Mayan ruins in Uxmal, which include massive stone structures.

103
Yleana

You can almost feel what it would have been like for the Mayans before the conquistadors.

The stunning, huge Mayan ruins at Uxmal rise far above the treetops.

hollowed-out Edam cheese," Baker tells us. "The soft part of the cheese, the center, was scooped out by the *patrón,* the boss. The servants got the rind, which they stuffed and steamed."

Baker says that Reyna Gallegos, her friend's Mayan cook, makes a fantastic *queso relleno* and she arranges for her to cook with Quintana the next afternoon. So in the morning, Quintana and I head to Izamal, a colonial town built on top of the ruins of a Mayan city dedicated to the sun god, Kinich-Kakmó. After the Spanish invaded, they used the stones from the temples to build an ochre-hued cathedral. If you look at the floor, you can see a carved mazelike pattern, a hallmark of Mayan design. Around town, hulking Mayan ruins still stand, pyramids of gray punctuating the green landscape.

For lunch, Baker recommends the restaurant Kinich-Kakmó, which has a traditional oval Mayan hut in the back garden. There's a pleasant shaded garden, but we choose to stay inside, where two Mayan women are making tortillas over an open fire.

"You can see the irregular pieces of corn in the masa—you know this is stone-ground by hand," Quintana says. These tortillas, which taste of fresh toasted corn, smoky from the fire, are steamy and wonderful; they're delicious fried and served with the vinegary turkey *en escabeche.*

When we return to Hacienda Xcanatún, Gallegos is already in the kitchen, an apron tied over the elaborately embroidered *hipil* she made herself. Her Spanish, tinged with a musical Yucatán accent and riddled with Mayan words, is hard for me to understand. But it's easy to follow her deft hands as, over the next two hours, she scrubs and trims the cheese rind to leave only the thinnest shell, then fills it with a near-black mixture of ground beef, raisins, olives, almonds and spices that have been fried together until nearly caramelized. The stuffed cheese rind, wrapped in cheesecloth and banana leaves, is then steamed until the inside turns molten and runny. The *patrónes* didn't know what they were missing.

Before we eat, Gallegos stoops over the food she's prepared and pauses to recite a prayer in her low Yucatán patois. Half in Spanish and half in Mayan, her blessing—over the Dutch cheese—is fitting for a cuisine and a region that, over the centuries, have evolved into their own compelling hybrid of so many cultures.

BY MELISSA CLARK

Flowers bloom luxuriantly in the warm climate of the Yucatán.

A simple shrimp and avocado salad in a citrus dressing takes advantage of fresh local produce.

Yucatán Lime and Chicken Soup

6 SERVINGS

The fragrant limes that are abundant on the Yucatán peninsula make this soothing soup especially appealing.

- 4 medium tomatoes
- 1 large white onion, unpeeled, plus ½ cup minced onion, for garnish
- 21 garlic cloves, peeled (2 heads)
- 3 whole chicken breasts on the bone (about 1¼ pounds each)
- 3 quarts chicken stock, low-sodium broth or water
- 2 limes, zest finely grated and limes halved, plus wedges for serving
- 20 allspice berries
- 1 tablespoon dried oregano, preferably Mexican, plus more for sprinkling

Salt and freshly ground pepper

- 1 cup plus 2 tablespoons vegetable oil
- 6 large scallions, white and green parts, very finely chopped

Twelve 6-inch corn tortillas, cut into thin strips

- 2 banana chiles or jalapeños, seeded and minced

1. Preheat the oven to 500°. Arrange the tomatoes on a small rimmed baking sheet. Set the unpeeled onion in a pie plate with 6 of the garlic cloves. Roast the vegetables on the top rack of the oven until blackened on top and tender, about 10 minutes for the garlic, 20 for the tomatoes and 30 for the onion. Let cool slightly, then cut the onion in half. Press the tomatoes through a coarse strainer.

2. In a large saucepan, cover the chicken with the stock. Add the lime zest and lime halves, allspice, oregano, the remaining 15 garlic cloves and a pinch each of salt and pepper and bring to a boil over moderately high heat. Add the roasted onion, reduce the heat to low and simmer until the chicken is cooked through, about 30 minutes.

3. Transfer the chicken to a platter and let cool. Gently simmer the broth for 10 minutes, then strain. Wipe out the saucepan. Remove the chicken meat from the bones and tear it into thick shreds.

4. Heat 2 tablespoons of the oil in the saucepan. Add the scallions and roasted garlic; mash the cloves to a paste with a fork. Cook over moderately high heat until the scallions are browned, 4 minutes. Add the

strained tomatoes and simmer until the fat separates from the sauce, about 5 minutes. Add the strained broth and bring to a boil; reduce the heat to low and simmer for 10 minutes. Season with salt and pepper.

5. Meanwhile, in a large skillet, heat the remaining 1 cup of oil until shimmering. Add one-fourth of the tortilla strips and fry over moderately high heat, stirring occasionally with a slotted spoon, until golden brown, about 2 minutes. Transfer to a paper towel–lined baking sheet and season with salt. Repeat with the remaining tortilla strips, lowering the heat if the oil gets too hot.

6. Add the chicken to the broth and cook until heated through. Ladle the soup into bowls, top with the tortilla strips and sprinkle with oregano. Serve, passing lime wedges, minced onion and banana chiles at the table.

MAKE AHEAD The chicken soup can be prepared through Step 5 up to 1 day ahead. Refrigerate the broth and shredded chicken separately. Keep the fried tortilla strips in an airtight container.

WINE The acidic, citrusy notes in this soup call for a dry Australian Riesling with matching citrusy flavors.

Quintana gets tips from tortilla makers, who use corn stone-ground by hand, at Kinich-Kakmó restaurant.

Garlic-Rubbed Spareribs

6 SERVINGS

Patricia Quintana loves to roast meat and fish in banana leaves, which add flavor and keep food moist and succulent. She cooks pork spareribs that way, then serves them with warm corn tortillas and bowls of garnishes alongside. You can also shred the sparerib meat, mix it with the pan juices and the onions it was roasted with and use the combination as a filling for warm corn tortillas.

- ¼ cup plus 2 tablespoons annatto (achiote) seeds
- 16 garlic cloves, 10 halved
- 1 medium onion, coarsely chopped
- 2 tablespoons dried oregano, preferably Mexican
- 2 tablespoons freshly ground pepper
- ½ cup fresh grapefruit juice
- ½ cup fresh orange juice
- ½ cup vegetable oil
- 3 racks large pork spareribs (about 3½ pounds each), trimmed of excess fat

Kosher salt

- 6 banana leaves, about 12-by-18 inches each (optional; see Note), thawed and patted dry
- 18 bay leaves
- 3 small red onions, thinly sliced

Two dozen 6-inch corn tortillas

Pickled Red Onions (recipe follows)

Yucatán Table Sauce (recipe, p. 38)

1. In a small saucepan, cover the annatto seeds with water, bring to a boil and simmer over moderate heat for 3 minutes. Remove from the heat and let stand for 2 hours. Drain the seeds and pat dry with paper towels. Transfer to a spice grinder and grind to a paste.

2. Preheat the oven to 500°. Put the 6 whole garlic cloves in a pie plate and roast on the top rack of the oven for 10 minutes, or until blackened on top. In a food processor, puree the roasted garlic with the halved garlic cloves and the onion. Add the annatto paste, oregano, pepper, grapefruit and orange juices, and oil and process until blended.

3. Rub the spareribs with 2 tablespoons of kosher salt. Set 1 of the racks in a large roasting pan and coat with one-third of the annatto marinade. Repeat with the remaining ribs and marinade, stacking the racks on top of each other. Cover with plastic wrap and refrigerate for at least 4 hours or overnight.

4. Preheat the oven to 350°. Line each of 3 large rimmed baking sheets with a banana leaf. Set a rack of ribs on each leaf, meaty side up. Arrange 6 bay leaves and one-third of the red onion slices on each rack and cover with a second banana leaf. Cover each pan tightly with foil and bake for about 2½ hours, or until the ribs are very tender; shift the pans halfway through cooking. Remove the spareribs from the oven and let cool, covered, for 15 minutes. Meanwhile, wrap the tortillas in foil and warm in the oven for about 10 minutes.

5. Preheat the broiler. Uncover the ribs and discard the banana leaves, onions and bay leaves. Broil the ribs, 1 rack at a time, about 8 inches from the heat, for 4 minutes, until crispy; baste occasionally with the pan juices.

6. Cut the racks into ribs and serve with the warm tortillas and bowls of Pickled Red Onions and Yucatán Table Sauce.

NOTE Banana leaves are available in the freezer section of Latin and Asian markets and can be found in the fresh produce section of some supermarkets.

MAKE AHEAD The recipe can be pre-pared through Step 3; refrigerate overnight.
WINE OR BEER A spicy, fruity Califor-nia Zinfandel will have the intensity to balance the meaty ribs. A dark Mexican beer is also fruity enough to stand up to the hearty grilled flavors.

Pickled Red Onions

MAKES ABOUT 1 QUART

This simple, piquant condiment is wonderful with grilled or baked meat or seafood, includ-ing Garlic-Rubbed Spareribs, p. 37.

Kosher salt

2½ quarts water

5 medium red onions, thinly sliced crosswise

½ cup extra-virgin olive oil

10 bay leaves

10 allspice berries

6 marjoram sprigs

1½ tablespoons dried oregano, preferably Mexican

1 teaspoon freshly ground black pepper

½ cup cider vinegar

1. In a large bowl, dissolve 2 tablespoons of salt in the water. Add the onions, let soak for 10 minutes and drain well.

2. Heat the olive oil in a large skillet. Add the onions, bay leaves, allspice, marjoram, oregano and pepper and cook over moder-ately high heat, stirring, until the onions are tender, about 10 minutes. Remove from the heat and stir in the vinegar. Season with salt and let cool. Discard the allspice, marjoram and bay leaves before serving.

MAKE AHEAD The pickled onions can be refrigerated for up to 1 week.

Shrimp and Avocado Salad with Citrus Dressing

6 SERVINGS

2 pounds large shrimp, shelled and deveined

¼ cup fresh grapefruit juice

1 tablespoon fresh lime juice

1 tablespoon cider vinegar

¼ teaspoon dried oregano, preferably Mexican

Salt and freshly ground pepper

6 medium tomatoes, thinly sliced crosswise

2 ripe Hass avocados—halved, peeled and sliced crosswise ¼ inch thick

1 medium red onion, thinly sliced crosswise

Extra-virgin olive oil, for drizzling

1. Bring a large saucepan of salted water to a boil over high heat. Cook the shrimp in the boiling water until they are loosely curled and just cooked through, about 2 minutes. Drain well; transfer the shrimp to a large bowl and let them cool slightly.

2. In a small bowl, combine the grapefruit juice and lime juice with the cider vinegar and dried oregano and season the citrus dressing with salt and pepper.

3. Add 2 tablespoons of the citrus dressing to the cooled shrimp, toss well and season with salt and pepper. Season the tomatoes and avocado slices with salt and pepper and arrange them on a serving platter with the sliced red onion, alternating and overlapping the slices. Spoon the remaining citrus dress-ing over the salad and top with the shrimp. Drizzle olive oil over the entire salad and serve immediately.

WINE A lively, crisp New Zealand Sauvi-gnon Blanc will have enough acidity to stand up to the sharpness of the tomatoes and vinaigrette, and still accent the shrimp.

Yucatán Table Sauce

MAKES ABOUT 1 CUP

This all-purpose hot sauce is called *xnipek*, or dog's nose, because it's so spicy it makes your nose as moist as a dog's. It is prepared with two kinds of chiles, including fiery habaneros.

2 jalapeños

4 scallions, white and green parts, very finely chopped

3 habanero or Scotch bonnet chiles, seeded and thinly sliced crosswise

½ cup coarsely chopped cilantro leaves

½ cup fresh grapefruit juice

¼ cup fresh orange juice

¼ cup fresh lime juice

Salt

1. Roast the jalapeños directly over an open flame or under a preheated broiler, turning occasionally, until blackened all over. Put the charred jalapeños in a small bowl, cover them with plastic wrap and let stand for 5 minutes. Discard the blackened skins, stems and seeds, then cut the jalapeños into thin strips.

2. In a bowl, combine the jalapeño strips with the chopped scallions, sliced habaneros, chopped cilantro and grapefruit, orange and lime juices. Stir the table sauce and season with salt.

MAKE AHEAD The sauce can be refrig-erated for up to 1 week.

Chile-Herb White Rice

6 SERVINGS

- 1 small onion, coarsely chopped
- 3 garlic cloves, halved
- 3 tablespoons vegetable oil
- 2 cups long-grain rice
- 3 cups water
- 2 teaspoons kosher salt
- 6 flat-leaf parsley sprigs, plus
  2 tablespoons chopped parsley
- 1 large jalapeño, 1 half cut into
  6 slices, the other half minced

1. In a mini processor, puree the onion and garlic. In a medium saucepan, heat the oil. Add the puree and cook over moderately high heat, stirring, for 1 minute. Add the rice and cook, stirring, for 1 minute. Stir in the water and salt and bring to a boil. Add the parsley sprigs and jalapeño slices, cover and cook over low heat for 25 minutes.

2. Remove the pan from the heat. Let stand, covered, for 30 minutes. Uncover the rice; wipe the lid dry. Discard the parsley sprigs and jalapeño slices; fluff the rice. Transfer the rice to a bowl, garnish with the chopped parsley and minced jalapeño and serve.

Melted Edam with Beef

6 TO 8 SERVINGS

Thanks to the Dutch presence in the Yucatán, Edam is ubiquitous at local markets. A whole aged cheese is often stuffed with ground meat and steamed, then served with two sauces: tomato-chile and creamy white. In the U.S., where cheese rinds aren't as sturdy, it's easier to shred and bake the cheese, then top it with the ground meat.

- ¼ cup pure olive oil
- 6 medium garlic cloves, very finely chopped
- 2 Anaheim chiles, coarsely chopped
- 1 white onion, coarsely chopped
- 1 large tomato, coarsely chopped
- 1 pound ground beef

Salt and freshly ground pepper

- ¾ cup pitted green olives, coarsely chopped
- ¾ cup golden raisins (4 ounces)
- ¼ cup drained capers
- 2 large hard-cooked egg yolks, finely chopped
- ¾ pound Edam cheese, shredded

1. Preheat the oven to 400°. In a medium skillet, heat the olive oil. Add the garlic, chiles and onion and cook over moderate heat, stirring, until the garlic and onion are lightly browned and softened, about 12 minutes. Add the tomato and cook for 1 minute, then push the mixture to 1 side of the skillet. Add the ground beef to the skillet. Break it up with a wooden spoon and cook over moderately high heat, stirring, until the beef starts to brown, about 4 minutes. Stir in the tomato mixture, season with salt and pepper and cook over moderate heat until the meat is cooked through, about 4 minutes.

2. Add the green olives, golden raisins and capers to the skillet and cook, stirring, until heated through, about 3 minutes. Add the egg yolks, season with salt and pepper and keep warm.

3. Spread the shredded Edam cheese in a large, shallow baking dish. Cover with foil and bake until just melted, 10 minutes. Spoon the beef mixture on top and serve immediately.

SERVE WITH Warm corn tortillas and Yucatán Table Sauce (recipe, p. 38).

TRAVEL TIPS

RESTAURANTS AND CAFÉS

- DULCERÍA Y SORBETERÍA COLÓN This chain of cafés, founded in 1907, serves delicious soft meringue cookies and sorbets like *elote,* made with nutty corn (Calle 62 #500, Mérida; 011-52-999-928-1497).
- KINICH-KAKMÓ Located near the cathedral, with tortillas handmade on the premises (Calle 27 #299, Izamal; 011-52-988-954-0489).
- LA PROSPERIDAD Specializes in small snacks called *botanas,* such as chicken-tortilla soup, and features a live band that plays Mexican pop (Calle 53 #491, Mérida; 011-52-999-924-1402).
- LOS ALMENDROS Homey restaurant in the center of Mérida that has excellent *salbutes*—crisp tortillas topped with turkey, tomatoes and onions (Calle 50 #57, facing Parque Mejorada, Mérida; 011-52-999-928-5459).

BOBBY FLAY
Scotland

Chef Bobby Flay, of New York City's Mesa Grill, works up an appetite at Turnberry golf course in Ayrshire. He satisfies his hunger on a tour of Arran Island, OPPOSITE, where Scottish chefs buy high-quality products like the cheeses from Island Cheese Company.

t's a brisk afternoon at Glasgow Gailes links in Ayrshire, a windswept county in southwestern Scotland, and Bobby Flay and I are teeing off. Flay is, of course, the famously redhaired, quick-tempered proselytizer for bold American cuisine, chef at New York City's Mesa Grill and Bolo, host of the Food Network's *Hot Off the Grill*—and, equally important, a keen golfer. We have come to Scotland to seek out fresh ingredients and distinctive local foods to fashion into recipes, and to look for great golf. During a few days' pleasant rambling, we turn up both.

We're just off the plane, and Flay hits a drive that cleaves the fairway and then, suddenly, hit by the wind, sails 40 yards to the right into a thicket of heather. He tees another ball, aiming farther left, but the wind flings this offering out of bounds too. Welcome to Scotland.

Our caddies, a father-and-son pair named Allan and Dave Queen, take us firmly in hand, telling us where to aim every stroke. "I'm the attractive one," Dave explains, "the one with teeth." His father conspicuously lacks incisors. In Scotland, where the favored foods are sugar, cream and lard, teeth go early, and so does the waistline. Beefy gents, called "salad dodgers," can be seen striding along at local links, staving off their appointed heart attacks. (Glasgow leads the world in cardiac arrests.)

"If you're serving everything to everybody, you're serving nothing to nobody."

BOBBY FLAY

Flay's creamy turnip soup with Parmesan and Asiago crisps was inspired by a Scotch broth.

Flay absorbs details about Arran produce from farmer Robin Gray on Arran Island.

Our first attempt to link golf and food is a total washout. The morning after our arrival, we have an 8 A.M. tee time at Prestwick, a handsome layout of narrow, crooked holes that was host to the first nine British Opens. When there turns out to be no breakfast at the club, we try the three hotels across the road. There doesn't seem to be anyone alive there, let alone anyone willing to rustle up Scotch eggs (the traditional bolus of a hard-boiled egg swaddled in sausage and deep-fried). Hungrily, then, we head out at Prestwick with the club's chef, a burly fellow who should probably remain nameless. At the first hole, Flay hits a four-iron that leaks into the rough. "You're swinging too fast," Nameless announces. Flay raises an eyebrow but says nothing. Then Nameless turns and informs me, "You're teeing it too high." Flay deftly changes the subject by asking Nameless polite questions about food. The answers he gets are generic. (Q: "What do you cook for the members?" A: "Everything from burgers to chicken tempura.") Over lunch later—which we have elsewhere—Flay says, "I could tell right away that Nameless was a shoemaker, a hack. When I asked about grouse, which is so Scottish, all he said was, 'Yeah, I cook it.' I mean, give me something—a sauce, a technique! He was all over the place, unfocused, with his burgers and his chicken tempura. If you're serving everything to everybody, you're serving nothing to nobody." Then Flay turns his attention to the Scotch broth we've ordered, a barley soup thickened with turnips and other vegetables. "This is good," he says, scraping the bowl. He is as focused on his meal as a small boy.

The next morning finds us walking on the pebbled shingle of Arran Island. An hour's ferry ride off the coast, Arran is a rural retreat that supplies Scottish chefs with fantastically fresh and distinctive produce, meat and cheeses. Though it encompasses 200 square miles of emerald hills and dales, Arran is home to only 4,500 people, many of whom still farm. Our guide here is Robin Gray, a former chef who grows organic herbs and vegetables, from lemon verbena to mizuna, along the shoreline. Gray has a kindly, rather eccentric manner. Having failed his driving test three times, he hitchhikes, or just plain hikes, to get around.

Gray explains how he fertilizes his turnips and arugula with seaweed gathered from this very beach: "It's the old way." Spotting a speckled oystercatcher's egg in the rocks, he says, "Ever have a seagull egg for breakfast? No?" His eyes light up. "You get a seagull egg, put a

After returning home, Flay created this crispy smoked-salmon hash with poached eggs and salmon caviar.

We have come
to Scotland to seek
out fresh ingredients
and distinctive
local foods to fashion
into great recipes,
and to look
for great golf.

Golfers in Scotland play on some of the world's
best courses while taking in beautiful views.

truffle next to it for a few days so that the truffle flavor seeps through the shell, then fry the egg and dip asparagus in it!"

"When Robin talks about a recipe, you can taste the meal," Flay says to me later. Formal restaurants in Ayrshire tend to serve roast beef and Dover sole—the Westin Turnberry Resort does classic food particularly well—but Gray also appreciates the subtle distinctions that underpin more innovative cuisine. When we visit Geoff Brookes' South Bank Farm Park to look at rare breeds of sheep, such as the runty but impressively named Castlemilk Moorits, Gray observes that sheep taste best in the brief "hogget" phase between 12 and 15 months, when the meat still has the tenderness of lamb but has taken on some of the flavor of mutton. Gray tells us that the Castlemilk Moorits "have a small carcass but a wonderfully gamey flavor—not like those blandies you get at the supermarket."

Brookes, a grizzled character whose waders are tied to his belt with orange string, stops by a pen where five Vietnamese pot-bellied piglets are rooting enthusiastically at their mother's teats. "How'd you enjoy those suckling pigs I sold you?" he asks Gray slyly. This is clearly an ongoing conversation between them.

Gray looks sheepish. "Well, I started to rub baby oil on them, to keep their skin soft. And then they would come up and just look at me."

"You're losing flavor every day."

"They're so small and affectionate," Gray says. "I can't kill them." Brookes rolls his eyes.

We stop at the docks to watch men dive for razor clams, then drive on to Creeler's Restaurant and Smokehouse, where the manager, Mark Williams, explains in boisterous detail

TRAVEL TIPS

HOW TO GET THERE
• Bobby Flay and writer Tad Friend flew to Glasgow on ICELANDAIR (800-223-5500). To get to Arran Island, they took an hour-long ferry trip from Ardrossan, which is about an hour from the Glasgow airport (011-44-1475-650-100). The Scottish tourist board is a good resource for travel information (800-969-7268).

WHERE TO STAY
• ARTHOUSE HOTEL, the latest modernist addition to Glasgow, has a staff that look like extras on *Sex and the City* (129 Bath St.; 011-44-141-221-6789; doubles from $220).
• WESTIN TURNBERRY RESORT, Golf Courses and Spa not only has the best golf course in the area, but it also has an extremely decorous staff (the concierges wear morning coats) and a bagpiper who plays in full regalia at sunset (Maidens Rd., Ayrshire; 011-44-1655-331-000; doubles from $260).

WHERE TO EAT
• CREELER'S RESTAURANT AND SMOKEHOUSE is Arran Island's best. Its smoked salmon is available by mail order (Home Farm, Brodick; 011-44-1770-302-797). The nearby Island Cheese Company features local products, including a great Scotch-flavored Cheddar (Home Farm, Brodick; 011-44-1770-302-788).

WHERE TO GOLF
• GLASGOW GAILES has subtle, true-rolling greens and an abundance of gorse to claim errant shots (Gailes Rd., Irvine, Glasgow; 011-44-1294-311-347). PRESTWICK is tight and tricky, with sheep hollows for bunkers (2 Links Rd., Prestwick; 011-44-1292-477-404). The Ailsa course at TURNBERRY is a must for the avid golfer. Tee times are usually available only to guests at the hotel (Maidens Rd., Ayrshire; 011-44-1655-331-000).

Signs point the way to great food on Arran Island.

the craft of smoking salmon: how he coats the fillets in coarse salt and molasses sugar until they surrender 8 percent of their weight, then cold-smokes them using ground-up whiskey-barrel shavings as fuel. "Try this," he says, handing us an orange slab of fish fresh from the oven.

"It's incredibly moist," Flay marvels. I can tell he's considering how to fit salmon into his menu.

Across the way is the Island Cheese Company, a tiny, tidy place that sells local farmers' cheeses—with their names pinned proudly to the wheels—and other Ayrshire foods. Flay picks up a jar of Hot Crunchy Mustard and says, "I love the sound of that." We have a taste—it's pungent, studded with whole mustard seeds. Then, with a furrowed brow, he tastes a half dozen goat cheeses, inquiring how long each has been aged. He favors the 10-week-old wheel, as it's more intense than the younger ones. He spends even longer selecting among the Cheddars. These are more buttery than their American counterparts, and many of them are flavored with chives, mustard or whisky. It's a fast way to get full, if a slow way to get drunk.

That night, over an excellent dinner of scallops, brown crab and lobster at Creeler's, Gray says, "Now, Bobby, here's a Scottish dessert for you: You take some Philadelphia cream cheese—"

"No way," Flay says.

"Bear with me, bear with me. You fill a meringue nest with cranachan—that's cream cheese mixed with fresh strawberries and raspberries, toasted oats and Scotch."

Flay leans forward. "Toast the oats?" he inquires.

"Just brown them lightly—ah, it's a treat."

Flay nods. "That would make a nice dessert—an oat cake with a warm berry compote, topped with clotted cream."

"With cream cheese," Gray says hopefully. Again, Flay raises a doubtful eyebrow.

The next day, back on the mainland, we head to the justly famed Ailsa course at Turnberry, the best links we play by far. But the bunkers are so steep and murderous that hitting out of them feels like digging your own grave; my ears are soon full of brown sand.

We like Turnberry so much we go back three times. On the final go-round, my caddie is Ian Milligan, another chesty fellow with bad teeth. For more than 20 years he has watched Americans struggle with the wind and the rough, and it seems to have soured him. During the first three holes, as I play excellent golf, he says not an encouraging word. Then I hit one mediocre shot on the fourth hole, and he bellows like a stuck pig, "Ah, no, no, no, no!" Startled, I grow wayward, only to hear him mutter from time to time "Terrible" or "What's that, then?" On the tenth hole, he gives his head a doleful shake, as if washing his hands of me. Soon, as Flay did with the local food experts, I begin listening to only some of Ian's comments, relying on my own instincts. Before long, I am playing well again. Sometimes, as Flay's recipes show, you have to temper local knowledge with good old American bravado.

BY TAD FRIEND

Flay serves his oat cake with warm berry compote and clotted cream.

Creamy Turnip Soup with Cheese Crisps

4 SERVINGS

Inspired by the traditional turnip-laden Scotch broth and the delicate young root vegetables of Arran Island, Bobby Flay developed this sweet, silky soup.

- 2 tablespoons extra-virgin olive oil
- 1 large Spanish onion, chopped
- 2 garlic cloves, chopped
- 1 pound small turnips, peeled and coarsely chopped
- ½ cup dry white wine
- 4 cups chicken stock or canned low-sodium broth, plus more for thinning the soup
- 2 tablespoons minced scallions
- ½ cup crème fraîche

Salt and freshly ground pepper

Cheese Crisps (recipe follows), for serving

1. Heat the olive oil in a large saucepan until shimmering. Add the chopped onion and garlic and cook over moderately high heat, stirring occasionally, until softened, about 6 minutes. Add the chopped turnips and cook, stirring frequently, until crisp-tender, about 5 minutes. Add the white wine and cook until almost evaporated, about 5 minutes. Add the 4 cups of the chicken stock and bring to a boil. Reduce the heat to moderately low and simmer until the chopped turnips are tender, about 25 minutes longer.

2. Working in batches, puree the turnip soup in a blender or food processor, then strain it through a fine sieve. Return the turnip soup to a clean saucepan, stir in the minced scallions and cook the soup over moderate heat for 5 minutes. Whisk in the crème fraîche until fully incorporated; thin the soup with stock if necessary. Season the turnip soup with salt and pepper.

3. Ladle the turnip soup into shallow bowls and serve with the Cheese Crisps.

MAKE AHEAD The soup can be refrigerated overnight. Gently reheat.

Cheese Crisps

MAKES ABOUT 16 CRISPS

Almost any freshly grated melting cheese can be used to make these crisps, but sharper cheeses are the best foil for the sweetness of the creamy turnip soup.

- ½ cup freshly grated Parmesan cheese
- ½ cup freshly grated Asiago cheese
- 1 tablespoon all-purpose flour

Heat a large nonstick skillet. In a small bowl, toss the Parmesan and Asiago cheeses with the flour. Spoon level tablespoons of the cheese mixture at least 2 inches apart into the skillet. Flatten each mound of cheese into a 2½-inch round and cook the rounds over moderate heat until brown around the edges, about 2 minutes. Using a thin spatula, flip the cheese crisps and cook until golden brown. Transfer the cheese crisps to a plate and let cool.

MAKE AHEAD The cheese crisps can be stored in an airtight container for up to 2 days. Recrisp them in a hot oven shortly before serving.

Smoked-Salmon Hash with Dill Vinaigrette

4 SERVINGS

This deliciously crisp hash, made with Scotland's finest cold-smoked salmon, is wonderful on its own or served with poached eggs for brunch.

Arran Island, famous for its lamb, inspired Flay's dish of grilled lamb chops with blackberry relish.

½ pound center-cut Scottish
cold-smoked salmon, in 1 piece

1 red bell pepper

3 tablespoons minced dill

1 tablespoon plus 1 teaspoon fresh
lemon juice

1 tablespoon minced shallot

¼ cup plus 2 teaspoons extra-virgin
olive oil

Salt and freshly ground pepper

¾ pound Yukon Gold potatoes, cut
into ¼-inch dice

1 tablespoon drained
prepared horseradish

4 poached eggs, for serving

2 tablespoons salmon caviar

1. Cut the salmon crosswise into 1-inch strips. In a medium saucepan of boiling water, poach the salmon until just cooked through, about 2 minutes. Drain on paper towels and break into large flakes.

2. Roast the red bell pepper directly over a low gas flame or under the broiler, turning occasionally, until lightly charred all over, about 15 minutes. Transfer the bell pepper to a bowl, cover with plastic wrap and let steam for 15 minutes. Peel, core and seed the pepper. Cut into ¼-inch dice.

3. In a mini processor, puree 1 tablespoon of the minced dill with the lemon juice and minced shallot. In a slow, steady stream, add 2 tablespoons plus 2 teaspoons of the olive oil to the processor and blend until emulsified. Season with salt and pepper.

4. In a saucepan fitted with a steamer basket, bring 1 inch of water to a boil. Add the diced potatoes and cook until they are just tender, about 4 minutes. In a medium bowl, toss the potatoes with the roasted bell pepper, flaked salmon, horseradish and the remaining 2 tablespoons of minced dill. Season the hash with pepper.

5. Heat a large cast-iron skillet. Add the remaining 2 tablespoons of olive oil and heat until shimmering. Add the salmon hash mixture to the skillet in an even layer and fry the salmon hash over moderately high heat until it is golden and crisp on the bottom, about 3 minutes. Scrape up the salmon hash and turn; continue frying until the hash is golden and crisp all over, about 8 minutes longer. Season the hash with salt and pepper and transfer to plates. Top the smoked salmon hash with the poached eggs, drizzle with the vinaigrette and garnish with the salmon caviar. Serve the hash at once.

Grilled Lamb Chops with Blackberry Relish

4 SERVINGS

Although berries and lamb are classic Scottish partners, this sweet-tart relish is also great with grilled pork, duck, beef or venison.

2 cups blackberries

2 tablespoons sugar

1 tablespoon chopped mint

1 tablespoon drained
prepared horseradish

1 tablespoon fresh lime juice

1 tablespoon extra-virgin olive oil,
plus more for brushing

Salt and freshly ground pepper

Eight 4- to 5-ounce loin lamb chops
(1 inch thick), trimmed

1. In a saucepan, cook the berries with the sugar over moderately high heat until the berries are softened but still hold their shape, 5 minutes. Transfer to a bowl; stir in the mint, horseradish, lime juice and the 1 tablespoon of oil. Season with salt and pepper; let cool.

2. Light a grill or preheat a grill pan. Brush the lamb chops with olive oil and season with salt and pepper. Grill over a medium-hot fire until medium rare, about 2 minutes per side. Serve with the blackberry relish.

Razor clams are harvested by hand off the coast of Scotland, then shipped around the world.

SERVE WITH Parslied boiled potatoes.

MAKE AHEAD The blackberry relish can be refrigerated for 2 days. Let return to room temperature before serving.

WINE An intense red, such as a California Merlot or a Châteauneuf-du-Pape from the Rhône, will stand up to the pungent lamb and echo the tart blackberries.

Oat Cake with Warm Mixed-Berry Compote

9 SERVINGS

A staple of the Scottish diet, rolled oats add a pleasant nutty flavor to cakes, biscuits, cookies and other simple desserts. For a lovely, dense and moist texture, use regular rolled oats rather than the instant or quick-cooking kind.

1 **cup rolled oats**

1¼ **cups boiling water**

1½ **cups all-purpose flour**

1 **teaspoon baking soda**

1 **teaspoon cinnamon**

¼ **teaspoon freshly grated nutmeg**

¼ **teaspoon salt**

1 **stick (4 ounces) unsalted butter, softened**

1 **cup packed light brown sugar**

½ **cup granulated sugar**

2 **large eggs**

1 **teaspoon pure vanilla extract**

Warm Mixed-Berry Compote (recipe follows)

Clotted cream, for serving

1. Preheat the oven to 350°. Butter and flour a 9-inch-square cake pan. In a heatproof bowl, soak the oats in the boiling water for 20 minutes. Drain well.

2. In a medium bowl, sift the flour with the baking soda, cinnamon, nutmeg and salt. In a large bowl, using a handheld electric mixer, beat the butter until creamy. Add the brown and granulated sugars and beat until light and fluffy. Beat in the eggs, 1 at a time, then beat in the vanilla. Add the soaked oats and beat at medium speed just until combined. At low speed, beat in the dry ingredients.

3. Scrape the batter into the prepared pan and bake the cake in the middle of the oven for 40 minutes, or until a toothpick inserted in the center comes out clean. Let cool in the pan for 10 minutes. Invert the pan, turn the cake out onto a wire rack; let cool completely.

4. Cut the oat cake into squares and serve with the Warm Mixed-Berry Compote and clotted cream.

Warm Mixed-Berry Compote

MAKES ABOUT 3 CUPS

1½ **cups fresh orange juice**

3 **tablespoons mild honey**

1 **large vanilla bean, split**

1½ **cups blueberries**

1½ **cups blackberries**

1½ **cups raspberries**

1 **tablespoon cornstarch dissolved in 1½ tablespoons water**

In a medium saucepan, combine the fresh orange juice with the mild honey. Scrape the seeds from the vanilla bean into the saucepan and then add the bean to the saucepan. Bring the flavored orange juice to a boil over moderate heat, stirring to dissolve the honey, about 2 minutes. Add the blueberries and blackberries and cook just until they are softened, about 2 minutes. Gently fold in the raspberries. Stir the cornstarch slurry and stir it into the compote in the saucepan. Simmer the berry compote until thickened and glossy, about 2 minutes. Discard the vanilla bean. Serve the mixed-berry compote warm.

MAKE AHEAD The mixed-berry compote can be refrigerated overnight. Reheat gently before serving.

MICHAEL LOMONACO
Mississippi

Michael Lomanaco, the chef at New York City's Guastavino's, followed signs for Highway 61, OPPOSITE, to find Mississippi Delta foods that would inspire his own inventions. Along the way he met Eddie Cusic, a local bluesman.

From the street, Turner's Grill, set amid a bleak cluster of shuttered storefronts in downtown Clarksdale, Mississippi, looks a bit intimidating. It seems as though most of the other buildings on the block closed a while back; a few may even have burned. But inside Larry and Lucille Turner's tidy café, the yellow walls glow as if backlit. A 75-watt bulb dangles above the gleaming steam table, illuminating today's feast: fried chicken, stewed chitlins, creamed potatoes and collard greens full of ham hocks and hot peppers. "This is the kind of place you wake up in the morning dreaming about," Michael Lomonaco says between bites of a drumstick sheathed in a ruddy crust. "If the blues gave birth to rock and roll—and we know they did in large part—then honest local food like this gave birth to what we now know as American cooking. Lomonaco, chef at Gustavino's in New York City, has come to explore one of the nation's most culturally rich and economically destitute regions: the Mississippi Delta, a 200-mile-long sliver of bottomland that hugs the Mississippi River from Memphis, in the north, to Vicksburg, Mississippi, in the south. Rather than trying to take in the whole stretch, Lomonaco hopes to see as much of the Mississippi triangle mapped out by Clarksdale, Greenwood and Greenville as one short weekend will allow. For Lomonaco the trip is a pilgrimage to the source of two things he reveres: simple

55

Mississippians adore their tamales, OPPOSITE,
introduced to the region by Mexican migrant workers.

Southern road food: donuts, tamales (note the warning on Orsby's tamale-mobile) and barbecue, OPPOSITE.

American food and the Delta blues. "Ever since I was a teenager and bought my first Lightnin' Hopkins album, I've been fascinated by blues music," Lomonaco says. "I even play a little guitar myself. And how could I not love the cooking? For me the Delta is the homeland of soulful food and music."

After we leave Turner's, our first stop is the Delta Blues Museum, set in an old redbrick freight depot. Clarksdale, a town just awakening to the possibilities of cultural tourism, can lay claim to a long and heady musical history. Bluesman Muddy Waters got his start nearby. Ditto John Lee Hooker, Son House, Ike Turner and a host of others. The museum, filled with vintage guitars, battered harmonicas and stunning black-and-white photographs of the local countryside, is worthy of an afternoon of study and reflection. It's also the unofficial welcome center for blues pilgrims, the place to stop when you need to know what juke joints are going to be hopping come the weekend. On the way out the door, Lomonaco picks up a couple of tips: There should be some music in an old commissary near Bourbon tonight, and California bluesman Bilbo Walker is supposed to play a homecoming set at a place called the Bobo Store on Saturday night.

Highway 61 beckons. Just one last stop before we leave town: Oscar Orsby's tamale-mobile. Each Friday and Saturday for the past 15-plus years, this seventysomething-year-old has parked his converted pickup at the corner of Fourth and Yazoo and set to work selling the Delta's favorite snack food to anyone with a few quarters jangling in his pocket. Lomonaco orders a half dozen for the road. "Now, be careful you don't eat your fingers right off," Orsby teases, handing over the greasy bundles. "I don't have insurance to cover you."

Migrant Mexican cotton pickers introduced hot tamales to the Delta during the early 20th century, but today few locals ponder matters of origin. Contrary to popular perception, the Delta is not just a land of West African and Anglo-Saxon cultures. In Clarksdale the best buttermilk biscuits are baked at Chamoun's Rest Haven, a Lebanese-owned roadside restaurant. The tastiest pork rinds are fried by the Wongs, a second-generation Chinese American family originally from the Guangdong province. After a few days in the Delta, you come to realize that hot tamales are as much a part of the culture as cotton and catfish.

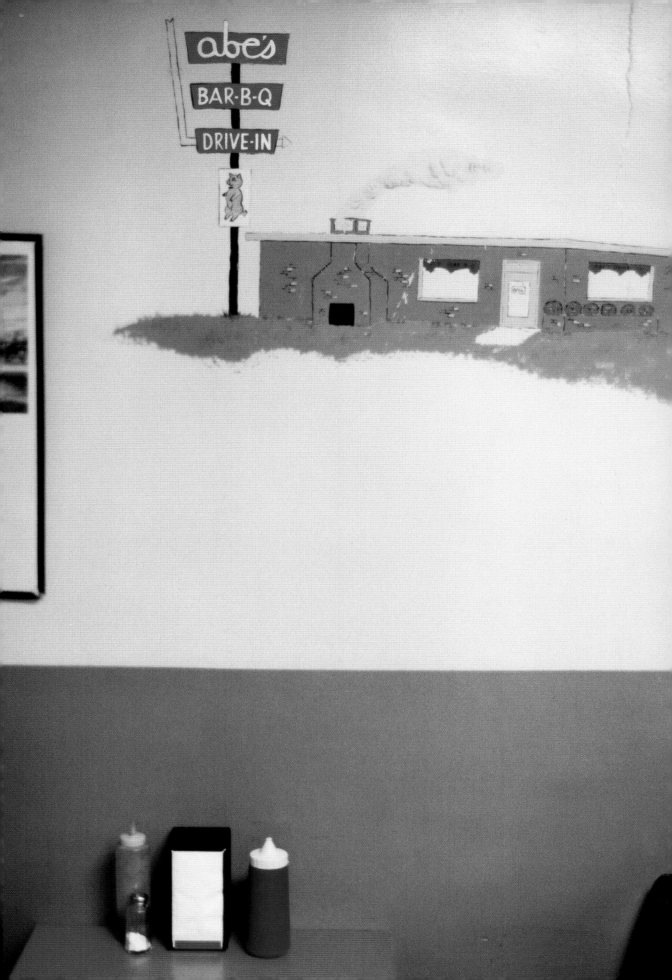

At last we're headed south down Highway 61, the same road once traveled north-ward by legions of black Mississippians seeking better jobs in St. Louis and Chi-cago, Detroit and New York, and freedom from the constraints of the Jim Crow South. The Delta rolls by along a ribbon of asphalt. Crossroad towns pass in quick succession, smudges of color glimpsed against a backdrop of dusky green cotton plants, their white bolls yet to blossom. Less than 150 years ago, the Delta was a swampy forest studded with cypresses. But generations of farmworkers—first slaves, later sharecroppers and day laborers—wrung out the land like a dish towel and ironed it flat. Today, when the sun sinks low in the sky, even dirt clods cast shadows.

Somewhere east of Leland, we leave the highway. Two wrong turns follow in quick suc-cession: dirt-lane dead ends. Though he is a native of Brooklyn, more accustomed to navi-gating the subway tunnels of New York than the two-lane blacktops of the rural South, Lomonaco drives on, bound for the Bourbon Mall Restaurant, known to everybody around here as Sonny's. At last he finds it, a funky little joint in an old clapboard building deep in the cotton fields outside the tiny community of Bourbon. We arrive to see local blues musician Eddie Cusic onstage, strumming a guitar. "Lord, I wish I was a catfish swimming in the deep blue sea," Cusic moans. "Lord, I'd have all these pretty women fishing after me."

The next morning, we chart a path along Highway 1, the Great River Road. On our left, groves of pecan trees. Come fall, the sweet brown nuts will blanket the ground and pecan pie will pop up on every café menu in the state, but for now clusters of small green husks hang heavy in the trees. On our right, the levee, and beyond, the churning brown waters of the mighty Mississippi River. Above, crop dusters trace colorful arcs through the sky, swooping low and slow over the cotton fields, trailing plumes of pesticide.

Along the way, we pass a fishmonger selling his catch from the back of a pickup truck. In one of the coolers, a monstrous chucklehead catfish lies in icy repose. Lomonaco leans in to have a look. "That's the sign of a truly fresh fish," he says, pointing toward the ruby-red gills. We pick up catfish sandwiches for the road.

Late in the afternoon, we pull into Greenwood, home of Lusco's, the Delta's most venera-ble and idiosyncratic restaurant, open since 1933. But first an appetizer: At the corner of John-son and Main, we lurch to the curb beside a two-barrel oil-drum grill, billowing pecan-wood smoke. Proprietor Leroy "Spooney" Kenter, tongs in hand, greets Lomonaco with a half slab of ribs napped in a bright vinegar-based sauce. The charred pork slips from the bone with the slightest tug, and three ribs later, Lomonaco claps his newfound friend on the back. "Those were the best," he says. "And I love the sauce. It doesn't overwhelm the meat." Spooney accepts his compliments with aplomb. "They call me the rib doctor," he says with a shy smile.

Lusco's is about a mile down the street, but, oh, what a difference a mile makes. After a weekend of rough-and-tumble roadside dining, we feel supremely civilized sitting down at a linen-draped table in the rear of this onetime grocery. Long the haunt of wealthy Deltans who

Lomonaco's fried-catfish sandwich with chipotle mayonnaise, an homage to a Delta favorite.

After a few days in the Delta, you come to realize that hot tamales are as much a part of the culture as cotton and catfish.

In Missisippi, funky joints in old wooden buildings offer amazing blues and, often, tasty food.

make their way to the wrong side of the tracks for a little dining, drinking and slumming, Lusco's exudes a kind of wizened gentility. "Sure, the paint is peeling and one of the bathrooms is out on the back porch, but we like it that way," a regular says. "At Lusco's it's good food that matters." So when the waitress pulls the curtain back on our private booth, bearing bowls of lettuce drizzled with vinaigrette and laced with anchovies, followed by platters of broiled shrimp and cups of delicate crabmeat cocktail—not to mention toothsome Black Angus rib eyes and whole pompano, scored, grilled and swabbed with a searing vinegar sauce—our party of six offers up a collective swoon and digs right in.

It's a long haul back up Highway 49, past the Parchman Prison Farm, through Swan Lake and Tutwiler, but with John Lee Hooker wailing on the stereo, time passes quickly. We slow to a crawl outside the town of Bobo. Lomonaco rolls his window down and cocks his head to the side in hopes of hearing the yelp of an electric guitar. He jerks the wheel and we turn onto a narrow lane. In no time, we're pulling into the parking lot of the Bobo Store, also known as Anderson Grocery.

The screen doors up front are locked, but the back end of the building is pulsing with sound and light. We enter through an unmarked side door, make our way to the bar and order tall-boy beers. The windowless joint is in upheaval. Down front, bluesman Robert "Bilbo" Walker, attired in an electric blue suit, his wiry hair fixed into a pompadour, is belting out an old B. B. King number. "The thrill is gone," he cries. "Baby, it's gone away from me." Lomonaco looks around at the dancers writhing against a bleary neon backdrop, his face creased by a wide grin. "This is it, the real deal!" he shouts above the din. "The only thing that might make it better would be a couple of Oscar's hot tamales."

BY JOHN T. EDGE

TRAVEL TIPS

WHERE TO STAY
• THE SHACK UP INN (8141 Old Hwy. 49 S., Clarksdale; 662-624-8329), which bills itself as Mississippi's B&B—that's Bed and Beer—rents refurbished sharecropper cabins and has a funky-chic bar next door.

OTHER STOPS ON LOMONACO'S ITINERARY
• ANDERSON GROCERY, known locally as the Bobo Store (520 Bobo New Africa Rd., Bobo; no phone).
• BOURBON MALL RESTAURANT, also known as SONNY'S (105 Dean Rd., Bourbon; 662-68 6-4389).
• CHAMOUN'S REST HAVEN (419 State St., Clarksdale; 662-624-8601).
• DELTA BLUES MUSEUM (1 Blues Alley, Clarksdale; 662-627-6820).
• KIM'S PORK RINDS (417 Third St., Clarksdale; 662-627-2389).
• LUSCO'S (722 Carrollton Ave., Greenwood; 662-453-5365).
• OSCAR'S TAMALES (Yazoo and Fourth Sts., Clarksdale; no phone).
• TURNER'S GRILL in Clarksdale has closed since Lomonaco's visit.

sunflower mall

HALEY INSURANCE

49 **Abe's** 61
at the
Legendary
CROSSROADS
GET YOUR SOUVENIR ▾ T-SHIRTS HER

"Ever since I was a teenager and bought my first Lightnin' Hopkins album, I've been fascinated by blues music," Lomonaco says about the inspiration for his trip. He indulges his curiosity about the blues and Southern food at joints in small towns and in shacks surrounded by fields during a weekend of rough-and-tumble roadside dining.

MISSISSIPPI antique 5589

Roll of Honor

John F. Kennedy
President

Dr. Martin Luther King
Nobel Prize Winner

Robert F. Kennedy
Senator

"The Three that Set Us Free"

Pulled-Pork Tamales

6 TO 8 SERVINGS

People in the Delta are very serious about their tamales, which were introduced to the region decades ago by Mexican migrant workers. Big or small, hot or mild, steamed or stewed—every version is delicious. The leftover pork is great for making sandwiches.

- 1 large onion, coarsely chopped
- ½ cup ketchup
- ¼ cup honey
- ¼ cup red wine vinegar
- 2 tablespoons Worcestershire sauce
- 2 tablespoons ancho chile powder
- 2 large garlic cloves

Coarse salt and freshly ground pepper

One 3½-pound boneless pork
     shoulder roast, tied

Hot water

Espresso Barbecue Sauce (recipe, p. 68)

- 2 cups *masa harina* (see Note)
- ⅓ cup solid vegetable shortening
- 1¼ teaspoons baking powder
- 24 fresh corn husks (from about
     5 ears of corn), optional

1. In a food processor, combine the onion, ketchup, honey, vinegar, Worcestershire sauce, chile powder, garlic and 2 table-spoons each of salt and pepper and pulse until a smooth paste forms. Transfer the paste to a large resealable plastic bag. Add the pork roast, turning to coat it with the paste; seal the bag and refrigerate for at least 8 hours or overnight.

2. Preheat the oven to 325°. Set the pork in an enameled casserole and cover with the paste. Add 1 cup of water and bring to a sim-mer. Cover the casserole and roast the meat in the oven for 3½ hours, or until meltingly

tender; turn the roast occasionally and add more water if it is looking dry. Transfer the pork to a cutting board and let cool. Remove the strings and pull the meat into thick shreds. Transfer to a bowl and toss with ½ cup of the Espresso Barbecue Sauce.

3. Put the *masa harina* in a large bowl. Add 1½ cups of hot water in a thin stream and beat at low speed until a dough forms. Con-tinue beating at medium-low speed until the dough is cool, about 5 minutes. Add the shortening, 1 tablespoon at a time, beating well after each addition. Beat in the baking powder and 2 teaspoons of salt. Scrape the dough into a large bowl and fold in 2½ cups of the shredded pork.

4. Arrange the corn husks on a large work surface. Scoop about ¼ cup of the tamale filling into the center of each husk. Fold the ends of the husks over the filling, then roll the husks up to enclose the filling completely. Alternatively, wrap ¼ cup of tamale filling in a rectangle of foil, forming an oval shape, and twist the ends securely. Place the ta-males, seam side down, in a large steamer basket, in several layers if necessary.

5. Steam the tamales until the filling is firm, about 20 minutes. Serve the pulled-pork tamales piping hot, with the remaining bar-becue sauce on the side.

NOTE *Masa harina*, a flour made from corn that has been treated with lime, is used to make tortillas and tamales. It is available at most supermarkets.

MAKE AHEAD The tamales can be pre-pared through Step 4 and frozen for up to 1 month in a sturdy plastic bag.

BEER These tamales are best suited to a full-flavored beer, such as a brown ale.

Fried Catfish Sandwiches with Chipotle-Honey Mayo

8 SERVINGS

Some of the freshest catfish in the Delta is sold right out of the backs of pickup trucks.

- 1 cup all-purpose flour
- ½ cup coarse yellow cornmeal
- ½ cup fine white cornmeal

Kosher salt and freshly ground pepper

- 2 large eggs, beaten
- ⅔ cup milk
- 8 skinless catfish fillets
     (5 ounces each)
- 1 cup mayonnaise
- 3 canned chipotle chiles in adobo
     sauce, halved and seeded
- 2 tablespoons honey
- 2 tablespoons fresh lemon juice
- 1½ cups vegetable oil,
     for frying
- 16 slices firm-textured white
     bread, toasted
- 1 head Boston lettuce, cut into
     ½-inch strips
- 2 large beefsteak tomatoes,
     thinly sliced

1. Line a baking sheet with wax paper. Put ¾ cup of the flour in a shallow bowl. In a second shallow bowl, combine the yellow and white cornmeals with 1 teaspoon salt, ¼ teaspoon pepper and the remaining ¼ cup flour. In a third shallow bowl, beat the eggs with the milk. Dredge the catfish fil-lets, one at a time, in the flour; shake off any excess. Dip the fillets in the egg mixture and coat them completely with the cornmeal mixture. Set the fillets on the baking sheet and refrigerate until the coating is dry, at least 1 hour.

Oscar Orsby, LEFT, sells tamales curbside. At Lusco's, customers sit at linen-draped tables.

2. Meanwhile, in a mini food processor, combine the mayonnaise with the chipotles, honey and lemon juice and process until smooth. Transfer the mayonnaise to a bowl; cover and refrigerate.

3. Preheat the oven to 250°. Put ½ cup of the oil in a large, heavy skillet and heat until shimmering. Add 3 of the catfish fillets and fry over moderately high heat until golden and crisp on 1 side, 5 to 6 minutes. Carefully turn the fillets over, reduce the heat to moderately low and fry until golden, crisp and cooked through, about 6 minutes longer. Using a slotted spatula, gently transfer the catfish fillets to paper towels to drain, then transfer the fried fish to a baking sheet and keep warm in the oven.

4. Wipe out the skillet with paper towels and add another ½ cup of oil. Fry the remaining fish in 2 batches, changing the oil between batches. Season the fried catfish with salt.

5. Spread a generous tablespoon of the chipotle-honey mayonnaise on 8 of the toast slices. Top with the lettuce, fried catfish and sliced tomatoes. Cover with the remaining 8 slices of toast. Serve the sandwiches immediately, passing any remaining mayonnaise at the table.

MAKE AHEAD The recipe can be prepared through Step 2. Both the coated catfish fillets and the chipotle-honey mayo can be kept in the refrigerator overnight.

WINE This simple country fish fry will be well-balanced by a lively white wine, such as a Chardonnay or Prosecco.

Cornmeal-Fried Okra, Tomatillos and Tomatoes

6 TO 8 SERVINGS

Okra, a staple of Southern cuisine, happens to be the mascot of the Delta State University sports teams. Lomonaco prefers to buy small, young okra pods for frying, reserving larger okra pods for stews. When buying okra, look for unblemished, firm bright-green pods. To trim okra, slice off the stems without cutting into the pods.

- 1 cup coarse yellow cornmeal, preferably stone-ground
- ½ cup all-purpose flour
- 1½ teaspoons cayenne pepper

Coarse salt

- 1 cup buttermilk
- 1 large egg, beaten
- 1 pound small young okra, trimmed
- ½ pound cherry tomatoes, halved through the stem ends
- ½ pound large tomatillos, husked and cut into 1-inch wedges
- 2 cups vegetable oil, for frying

Hot sauce, for serving

1. In a large resealable plastic bag, combine the cornmeal, flour, cayenne and 2 teaspoons of salt. In a large, shallow bowl, whisk the buttermilk with the egg.

2. Dip the okra into the beaten egg and, using a slotted spoon, transfer it to the plastic bag with the cornmeal and flour mixture. Shake to coat completely, then transfer the okra to a large plate. Repeat with the cherry tomatoes and then the tomatillos.

3. Heat the oil in a large cast-iron skillet until it is shimmering. Fry the okra over moderately high heat, turning occasionally, until it is golden and crisp, 2 to 3 minutes. Using a slotted spoon, transfer the fried okra to paper towels to drain. Reheat the oil and fry the cherry tomatoes until golden and crisp, 2 to 3 minutes. Drain the tomatoes on paper towels. Reheat the oil and fry the tomatillos, then drain them. Gently toss the fried vegetables together, season them with salt and serve hot, with hot sauce on the side.

Shrimp on "Killed" Salad

6 SERVINGS

The fresh greens will wilt slightly under the hot shrimp. You might find that this recipe is prepared with crawfish instead of shrimp when it's served in a Southern tearoom or lunch parlor. For a more refined dish, shell the shrimp before marinating them.

- 5 tablespoons unsalted butter, melted
- 2 tablespoons sweet paprika
- 1 tablespoon unsulfured molasses
- 1 teaspoon dry mustard
- 1 teaspoon lemon pepper
- 1 teaspoon onion powder
- ½ teaspoon cayenne pepper
- ½ teaspoon ground cumin

Coarse salt

- 2 pounds large shrimp, butterflied through the back and deveined
- ¼ cup white wine vinegar
- ¼ cup dry white wine
- 2 tablespoons honey
- 2 tablespoons yellow mustard
- 2 tablespoons finely chopped parsley
- 1 tablespoon finely chopped garlic
- 1 tablespoon finely chopped anchovy fillets
- ⅓ cup extra-virgin olive oil, plus more for pan-grilling
- ½ pound sliced bacon
- 6 cups mixed greens, such as watercress and green leaf lettuce, torn into bite-size pieces
- 2 carrots, coarsely shredded

Freshly ground black pepper

1. In a medium bowl, combine the butter, sweet paprika, unsulfured molasses, dry mustard, lemon pepper, onion powder, cayenne, cumin and 1 teaspoon of salt. Lay the large shrimp, shell side down, on a baking sheet and brush the shrimp with the paste. If necessary, separate layers of shrimp with wax paper. Cover and refrigerate the shrimp for at least 1 hour.

2. In a blender, combine the white wine vinegar, white wine, honey, yellow mustard, and finely chopped parsley, garlic and anchovies and puree. With the machine on, add ⅓ cup of the olive oil in a thin stream and blend until the mixture is emulsified. Transfer the dressing to a jar.

3. In a large skillet, cook the sliced bacon over moderately high heat until browned and crisp, about 6 minutes. Drain the bacon on paper towels. Crumble the bacon into a large bowl. Add the mixed greens, shredded carrots and 2 tablespoons of the dressing; season the salad with black pepper and toss. Arrange the salad on 6 large plates.

4. Heat a cast-iron grill pan or a large skillet and coat lightly with olive oil. Add the shrimp in batches and cook over high heat, drizzling occasionally with some of the dressing and turning once, until bright pink and blackened in spots, 4 to 5 minutes. Arrange the shrimp on the salads and serve immediately. Pass the remaining dressing at the table.

MAKE AHEAD The recipe can be prepared through Step 2 and refrigerated overnight.

WINE The tanginess of this salad requires a match with enough acidity to hold its own. Try a white wine, such as a Pinot Blanc from Alsace or a Crozes-Hermitage Blanc from the Northern Rhône.

Espresso Barbecue Sauce

MAKES ABOUT 2 CUPS

Lomonaco contributes his own twist to this barbecue sauce by using espresso, which adds a jolt of rich flavor. The barbecue sauce works well with pork, beef and poultry, complementing and rounding out the flavor of meat.

- 1 large onion, finely chopped
- 2 large garlic cloves, very finely chopped
- ¾ cup packed dark brown sugar
- 1 cup red wine vinegar
- 1 cup ketchup
- 1 cup brewed espresso
- 3 tablespoons molasses
- 2 tablespoons dry mustard mixed with 1 tablespoon water
- ¼ cup ancho chile powder
- 2 tablespoons Worcestershire sauce
- 2 tablespoons ground cumin
- 1 teaspoon coarse salt
- 1 teaspoon freshly ground pepper

Combine all of the ingredients in a medium saucepan and simmer over moderately low heat, stirring occasionally, until the sauce has reduced by about half, about 45 minutes. Let the sauce cool completely then strain and puree in a blender until smooth. Serve the barbecue sauce right away or cover the sauce and refrigerate until ready to use.

SERVE WITH Pulled-Pork Tamales (recipe, p. 66), or any grilled meat.

MAKE AHEAD The Espresso Barbecue Sauce can be refrigerated in a covered jar for up to 3 months.

The Delta rolls by along ribbons
of asphalt and railway lines.

FRANCIS MALLMANN
Patagonia

Argentinean star chef Francis Mallmann (in vest) returns from his trout-fishing expedition. Later he grates potatoes with his daughter, Alexia, OPPOSITE, to make potato cakes stuffed with grilled trout.

f Argentinean cooking has a star, there's no question who it is: Francis Mallmann. The 49-year-old Patagonian is the only non-European winner of the International Academy of Gastronomy's Grand Prix de l'Art de la Cuisine. Thanks to his good looks, his boyish personality and, not least, his culinary skill, he has become a national TV presence of Emeril-like ubiquity and the force behind a string of successful restaurants—one in the capital, Buenos Aires; one in the Mendoza wine region; two on the coast of Uruguay, where the Argentinean elite migrates during the summer months; and one in the resort town where he was born, San Carlos de Bariloche, which might be described as the Jackson Hole of Patagonia.

People tend to think of Patagonia (if they think of it at all) as a place at the end of the earth. It's a region of wide plains and awe-inspiring peaks, a thousand-mile strip of Argentina and Chile that runs down the eastern spine of the Andes almost to the tip of South America. Historically this was the frontier, home to the bedaggered and billowy-trousered cowboys known as gauchos and to the Araucanian Indians, whom the Spanish never conquered. Today Patagonia has become popular with an international crew of winter skiers and summer anglers—a Wild West with Hermès scarves and Basque berets.

Meaty dishes like lamb in rosemary *chimichurri*,
OPPOSITE, are ideal for hungry fishermen.

Twice a year, Mallmann packs up his car and, with family and friends in tow, makes the 500-mile pilgrimage from his house in Bariloche to his rustic cabin on an island in the middle of an ice-blue, ice-cold mountain lake, where he has just six neighbors within a 50-mile radius. Or else he flies in to the tiny airstrip nearby, though usually he prefers the sinuous highway: "If you drop in by plane," he says, "your body gets there before your soul." It's the kind of observation a poet might make, and as a matter of fact, Mallmann has been gaining a following not just for his cooking but also for his sensual (actually, downright erotic) blank verse and short stories.

For most of us, Argentinean food means endless servings of barbecued meat with, perhaps, a few empanadas to start. Both are on the menu at Mallmann's restaurants as well as at his cabin, where he does much of his cooking outdoors. But the chef has traveled and studied extensively in Europe, including stints at Troisgros in Roane and Taillevent in Paris, and his graceful touch transforms these traditional dishes. He is known, in fact, for his highly sophisticated take on the food of the pampas. He makes much of the 600-degree clay empanada ovens at his restaurants: "They're descendants of Incan stoves," he explains, "and we use them for everything: We cook fish, roast game and bake pies in them in individual cast-iron boxes."

"I learned to cook properly in France," Mallmann says. "France has the best techniques in the world for cooking. But these days I like the food in Italy better, especially in the countryside. I don't like big, fussy restaurants anymore—my style is very simple now. I almost never use classic sauces, like béchamel. I don't make decorations, I don't make towers—I've been through all that. As you get older, you stop copying other people; you can be brave and start doing simple things."

Take his trout, for instance. Practically the first thing Mallmann does when he arrives at the cabin is string up his fly rod and catch a panful of trout, whose pink flesh is the hallmark of wildness. After he fillets and grills them, he layers them with *rösti* potatoes and spinach in a straightforward dish that's a staple at the cabin and at his restaurants, too. And his empanadas are a far cry from the wonton-like little things you see in the States: they're crispy, delectable dumplings filled with the savory onion, olive, egg and beef filling typical of the Mendoza region. (Every region has its preferred empanada filling.)

A similarly unfussy baby lamb, also a regular at the restaurants, shows off the virtues of *chimichurri*, the Argentinean condiment that, when it's freshly made, is the most brightening of all taste enhancers for meat. And *carbonada*—a pumpkin crammed full of veal, brisket, peaches, peppers and onions—is an inspired and fortifying dish that wards off the cold of the Andean nights. It's not bad on cold mornings, either, for the early risers who get up to join Mallmann down at the lake for the first trout of the day.

BY PETER KAMINSKY

Mallmann's Patagonian cabin is on an island in the middle of a lake; he sometimes lands nearby in a tiny plane. He can't wait to go fishing, after which he'll grill his dinner over an open fire. Dessert might be crêpes with caramel and sugar.

Wide plains
and awe-inspiring
peaks provide
the backdrop
for a rustic
lakeside dinner.

Mallmann sets a table overlooking
the ice-blue, ice-cold lake.

Roasted Lamb with Potatoes and Rosemary Chimichurri

6 SERVINGS

If you're a year-round griller, you can grill the lamb, as they do in Patagonia, instead of roasting it. The potent, garlic-accented *chimichurri,* the ubiquitous Argentinean accompaniment to grilled or roasted meat, is excellent with the charred lamb and buttery fried potatoes.

1   cup extra-virgin olive oil
½   cup rosemary leaves, finely
    chopped
1   head of garlic, minced
Finely grated zest of 1 lemon
2   tablespoons fresh lemon juice
½   teaspoon crushed red pepper
Kosher salt
One 5½-pound boneless leg of lamb,
    butterflied
Freshly ground black pepper
1   stick (4 ounces) unsalted butter
5   large Idaho potatoes, peeled and
    sliced ¼ inch thick

1. In a bowl, combine the oil, rosemary, garlic, lemon zest, lemon juice, crushed red pepper and 1 tablespoon kosher salt. Let the *chimichurri* stand at room temperature for at least 20 minutes.

2. Preheat the oven to 500°. Season the lamb with salt and pepper and brush on both sides with ⅔ cup of the *chimichurri.* Set the lamb, fat side up, on a large rimmed baking sheet and roast in the upper third of the oven for about 25 minutes, or until an instant-read thermometer inserted in the thickest part of the meat registers 130° for medium-rare. Transfer the lamb to a cutting board, cover with foil and let rest for 10 minutes.

3. Meanwhile, divide the butter between 2 large skillets, preferably cast-iron. Add one-quarter of the potatoes to each skillet and cook over low heat until browned on the bottom, about 15 minutes. Turn the slices with tongs and fry until browned on the other side, about 5 minutes longer. Transfer the potatoes to a rack set over a baking sheet and season with salt. Keep the potatoes warm on the back of the stove. Fry the remaining sliced potatoes.

4. Thickly slice the lamb. Arrange the fried potatoes on a plate, top with the lamb and spoon the *chimichurri* over it all.

MAKE AHEAD The *chimichurri* is best made 1 to 2 days ahead and refrigerated. Let the *chimichurri* return to room temperature before serving.

WINE A Cabernet Sauvignon from Chile will echo the fresh rosemary and match the gaminess of the lamb.

Beef and Veal Stew in Pumpkins

6 SERVINGS

This shredded meat stew, called a *carbonada,* is flavored with scallions and pancetta and served in large pumpkins. In season, Mallmann adds peaches to the mix. If you can't find pumpkins, acorn squash are a fine alternative.

2   meaty pieces of veal shank
    (1 pound each)
2   pounds of beef brisket, cut across
    the grain into 2 pieces
6   cups chicken stock or canned
    low-sodium broth
2   bay leaves
2   parsley sprigs
2   thyme sprigs
Salt and freshly ground black pepper
Two 5-pound pumpkins or 3 large
    acorn squash
2   tablespoons unsalted butter
½   cup milk
2   tablespoons olive oil
4   ounces thinly sliced pancetta,
    coarsely chopped
2   scallions, thinly sliced
3   ears of corn, shucked and cut into
    1½-inch rounds
3   medium onions, thinly sliced
1   red bell pepper, cut into
    ½-inch dice
1   teaspoon crushed red pepper

1. In a large saucepan, cover the veal and beef with the stock. Add the bay leaves, parsley and thyme, season lightly with salt and black pepper and bring to a boil over moderate heat. Reduce the heat to low, cover partially and simmer until the meats are very tender, about 2 hours for the veal and 3½ hours for the beef. As the meats are done, transfer them to a bowl and let cool slightly. Discard the bones and gristle. Cut the meats into 1-inch pieces. Strain the cooking liquid into a bowl; you should have about 2 cups.

2. Preheat the oven to 350°. Cut the tops off the pumpkins and reserve. Scrape out the seeds and season the insides of the pumpkins with salt and pepper. Add 1 tablespoon of the butter and ¼ cup of milk to each pumpkin, cover with the tops and set them on a rimmed baking sheet. Bake for 1¼ hours, or until the pumpkins are just tender. Cover with foil and keep warm. Alternatively, halve each acorn squash lengthwise and scrape out the seeds with a spoon.

Carbonada—a pumpkin filled with stewed veal and beef—can provide comfort on cold Andean nights.

Season the squash with salt and pepper and fill the centers with the butter and milk. Transfer the squash to a large baking dish and roast, cut side up, for about 30 minutes, or until tender; keep them warm in the dish.

3. In a large skillet, heat 1 tablespoon of the olive oil. Add the pancetta and cook over low heat, stirring often, until crisp, about 5 minutes. Stir in the scallions and transfer the mixture to a plate.

4. In a medium saucepan of boiling water, cook the corn until tender, about 5 minutes; drain.

5. In a large saucepan, heat the remaining 1 tablespoon of olive oil. Add the onions and bell pepper and cook over low heat until softened, about 10 minutes. Add the crushed red pepper and cook, stirring, for 1 minute. Add the meats and their cooking liquid, the pancetta mixture and corn and simmer until heated through, about 4 minutes. Season with salt and black pepper.

6. Spoon the stew into the pumpkins or squash. Cover the pumpkins with the tops, or cover the squash with foil; bake until heated through, about 20 minutes for the pumpkins and 10 minutes for the squash. Bring the stew to the table in the pumpkins, then spoon the stew into bowls, scooping out the pumpkin flesh. Alternatively, serve each guest a stew-filled squash half.

WINE Try a soft, round Chilean Merlot with this meaty stew.

Spinach and Ricotta Gnocchi

6 SERVINGS

It's a popular tradition in Argentina that gnocchi should be eaten on the 29th day of each month.

2 pounds fresh spinach—
   large stems discarded, leaves
   rinsed but not dried
3 large eggs
3 large egg yolks
1 cup whole-milk ricotta cheese
½ cup freshly grated Parmesan
   cheese, plus ¾ cup shavings
Kosher salt and freshly ground
   black pepper
¼ teaspoon freshly grated
   nutmeg
2 cups all-purpose flour
2 cups heavy cream
1 tablespoon minced sage, plus
   6 large leaves for garnish

1. Heat a skillet. Add the spinach by handfuls and cook over high heat, stirring, until just wilted. Transfer the spinach to a colander and press out the excess water. Finely chop the spinach.

2. In a large bowl, combine the spinach with the whole eggs, egg yolks, ricotta cheese, freshly grated Parmesan cheese, 2 teaspoons kosher salt, ¼ teaspoon black pepper and the nutmeg; stir well. Add the flour and stir just until combined; the dough will be soft and sticky.

3. Scoop out rounded teaspoons of the dough onto a well-floured work surface, and roll each piece into a ball. On lightly floured baking sheets, arrange the balls so they aren't touching.

4. Bring a large saucepan of salted water to a boil. In a medium saucepan, combine the cream and minced sage and simmer over low heat, stirring, until slightly thickened, about 12 minutes. Season with salt and pepper and keep warm.

5. Cook the gnocchi in the boiling water until they rise to the surface, about 5 minutes. Transfer the gnocchi to a shallow bowl. Pour the sage sauce over the gnocchi. Garnish with the sage leaves and Parmesan shavings and serve.

MAKE AHEAD The uncooked gnocchi can be refrigerated overnight, covered.

Grilled Chicken with Lemon-Herb Sauce

6 SERVINGS

1⅓ cups olive oil
⅓ cup red wine vinegar
3 garlic cloves, smashed
Grated zest of 1 lemon
1 tablespoon crushed red pepper
Six 7-ounce skinless boneless chicken
   breast halves, scored in a
   crosshatch pattern
2 tablespoons oregano leaves
2 tablespoons thyme leaves
Kosher salt
⅓ cup fresh lemon juice
Freshly ground pepper
4 large Idaho potatoes, peeled and
   cut into 1-inch dice
1 medium white onion, coarsely
   chopped
2 medium tomatoes, chopped

1. In a bowl, combine ½ cup of the oil with the vinegar, garlic, lemon zest and crushed red pepper. Add the chicken breasts and turn to coat evenly. Refrigerate for 1 hour, turning the breasts.

2. In a mortar, crush the oregano, thyme and ½ teaspoon of salt. Stir in the lemon juice and ⅓ cup of the olive oil and season with salt and pepper.

Water for maté is boiled on the wood-burning stove.

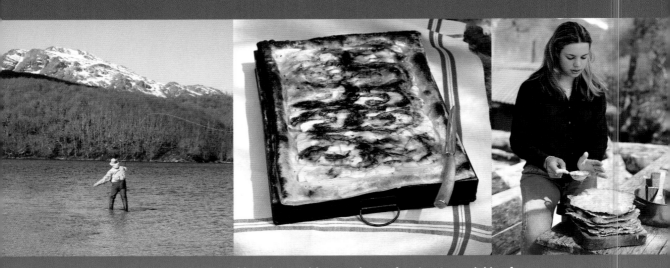

An apple tart is topped with a shiny glaze; *tableton* (crispy crêpes) get a sprinkle of sugar.

3. In a large cast-iron skillet, heat the remaining ½ cup of oil. Add the potatoes in an even layer and cook over moderate heat until browned on the bottom, about 15 minutes; lower the heat halfway through cooking. Stir the potatoes and cook until browned all over, about 10 minutes longer. Add the onion and cook over moderate heat, stirring, until beginning to brown. Season with salt and pepper.

4. Light a grill or preheat a grill pan. Remove the chicken from the marinade and season with salt and pepper. Grill the chicken over a moderately hot fire until charred and cooked through, about 5 minutes per side. Transfer to a platter.

5. Warm the potatoes over high heat; stir until sizzling. Add the tomatoes and cook, stirring, for 1 minute. Spoon the sauce over the chicken; serve with the potatoes.

Potato Cakes Stuffed with Trout

6 SERVINGS

Trout is a staple in Patagonia that's often served with potatoes. To remove the tiny pin bones, arrange a fillet, skin side down, on an upside-down bowl; the bones will stick out. Remove them with tweezers.

- 2 pounds medium all-purpose potatoes, scrubbed
- Salt and freshly ground pepper
- 4 skinless rainbow trout fillets, cut crosswise into 3 pieces
- About 1 stick (4 ounces) unsalted butter
- About ½ cup canola oil
- 12 baby spinach leaves, stems discarded

1. In a large saucepan, cover the potatoes with cold water and bring to a boil over high heat. Reduce the heat to moderate and cook the potatoes until their outsides are fork-tender but their centers are still hard, about 15 minutes. Drain and cool under running water. Peel the potatoes and coarsely grate them. Season with salt and pepper and toss to combine.

2. Season the trout with salt and pepper. On a cast-iron griddle or skillet, melt ½ tablespoon of the butter in ½ tablespoon of the oil. Spoon a scant ½ cup of shredded potatoes onto the griddle and flatten into a 5-inch round. Set a piece of trout in the center, cover with a spinach leaf and top with a scant ½ cup of potatoes, flattening them.

3. Cook the potato cake over moderately low heat until crispy and golden on the bottom, about 5 to 7 minutes. Using a spatula, carefully turn the potato cake and cook until the potatoes are crisp and golden and the trout is just cooked through, about 5 minutes longer; add more butter and oil if necessary. Transfer to paper towels to drain, then serve hot. Repeat with the remaining grated potatoes, trout and spinach leaves, serving the potato-trout cakes hot.

WINE Pick a Sauvignon Blanc–based wine from either California or New Zealand to provide a foil for this homey potato and trout dish.

Glazed Apple Tart

6 SERVINGS

- ½ pound store-bought all-butter puff pastry
- 2 tablespoons (1 ounce) unsalted butter, melted
- 2 large Granny Smith Northern Spy apples—peeled, halved, cored and sliced lengthwise ¼ inch thick
- 2 tablespoons granulated sugar

Patagonia, once known for bedaggered cowboys called gauchos, shows its luxurious side at this dinner.

1. Preheat the oven to 400°. Line a large baking sheet with parchment paper. On a lightly floured work surface, gently roll out the puff pastry to a 12-by-10-inch rectangle, that is about ⅛ inch thick. Using the rolling pin, carefully transfer the rolled out puff pastry to the baking sheet and brush the pastry with 1 tablespoon of the melted butter.

2. Arrange the apple slices on the puff pastry in 3 neat lengthwise rows, overlapping the slices slightly and leaving a ½-inch border all around. Brush the apple slices with the remaining 1 tablespoon of melted butter and sprinkle with 1 tablespoon of the granulated sugar. Bake the tart on the bottom rack of the oven for about 30 minutes, or until the pastry is cooked through and nicely browned all over. Remove the tart from the oven and preheat the broiler.

3. Sprinkle the apples with the remaining 1 tablespoon of granulated sugar and broil them for about 30 seconds, or until the apples start to brown on top; rotate the pan as necessary to prevent charring. Cut the apple tart into 6 large squares and serve at once.

Crisp Crêpes Filled with Caramel

6 SERVINGS

This supersweet dessert, called *tableton* in Argentina, consists of layers of crunchy pastry rounds and a rich caramel made simply by boiling milk and sugar until thickened and golden.

- 4 **large egg yolks**
- ½ **cup dessert wine, such as Marsala**
- 2 **cups all-purpose flour**
- 1 **quart whole milk**
- 2 **cups granulated sugar**
- 1 **vanilla bean, split lengthwise, seeds scraped**
- 2 **tablespoons confectioners' sugar**

1. In a large bowl, whisk the egg yolks with the wine. Stir in the flour. When the dough becomes too stiff to stir, transfer it to a floured work surface and knead in any remaining flour until smooth. Cover with plastic wrap and refrigerate until firm, about 2 hours.

2. In a saucepan, combine the milk, granulated sugar and the vanilla bean and scraped seeds. Bring the milk to a boil and simmer over moderate heat, stirring occasionally, until golden brown and reduced to 2 cups, about 1 hour. Transfer the caramelized milk to a bowl; discard the vanilla bean. Let the caramel stand, stirring often, until cooled.

3. Preheat the oven to 400°. Cut the dough into 8 equal pieces and shape each piece into a ball. Cover the balls of dough with a clean kitchen towel. On a lightly floured surface, roll out one ball of dough to an 8-inch round and transfer to a large baking sheet; repeat with another ball. Bake the dough for about 10 minutes, or until browned and crisp. Transfer the crêpes to a plate. Roll out and bake the remaining balls.

4. Place a crêpe on a cake plate. Using a metal spatula, spread a scant ¼ cup of caramel over the crêpe and set another crêpe on top. Repeat with the remaining caramel and crêpes; don't glaze the last crêpe. Sift the confectioners' sugar on top. Using a serrated knife, gently saw the stack into 6 wedges and serve.

MAKE AHEAD The crêpes can be stored in an airtight container for up to 1 day. The caramel should be refrigerated. Let the caramel return to room temperature before using.

ERIC RIPERT
Puerto Rico

On a road trip from San Juan to El Yunque, the Puerto Rican rain forest, four-star chef Eric Ripert (OPPOSITE), of Le Bernardin in New York City, stops at one of the fritter stands near the beach for a sip of cool coconut water.

The friendly Texan ladies next to me at the hotel bar are happily at work on identical plates of chicken quesadillas and french fries. Other dining options on the 17 acres that comprise the Caribe Hilton in San Juan include a Northern Italian restaurant, a Spanish tapas bar, a Chicago steak house and a dining room serving everyone's favorite cuisine, International. All of which should be enough to satisfy any normal tourist down from the mainland, but it is my misfortune to be plagued by visions of life outside the Hilton compound. I happen to know that elsewhere in Puerto Rico, suckling pigs are turning slowly over burning charcoal, plantains are swaying in hot fat, vats of red beans are murmuring on back burners.

What I need is a local guide. Somebody island-born and Spanish-speaking who knows the difference between *mofongo* and *mondongo,* and can tell them apart at 50 paces. Somebody with a gut that billows proudly before him like the front grille of a PT Cruiser.

What I've got is a skinny French guy. I'm in Puerto Rico with Eric Ripert, the chef at one of New York's greatest and most expensive restaurants, Le Bernardin. Normally you won't hear me complaining about hanging out with a man whose idea of a grilled cheese sandwich involves smoked salmon and sevruga caviar. In Manhattan, Eric Ripert can do no wrong. But

Ripert finds the inspiration for Jumbo Shrimp with
Garlic Butter in Puerto Rico's pristine seafood.

During his tour in Piñones, Ripert discovers the ingredients for Chorizo and Pinto-Bean Stew, OPPOSITE.

in San Juan? As soon as Ripert bounds into the bar, though, my chances of encountering red beans and suckling pig start to rise at a near-vertical incline. First, he tells me that he's been coming to Puerto Rico at least annually for at least 20 years. It's his favorite place to disappear to when things get to be too much, so he knows his way around. And he has spoken Spanish all his life—he grew up in Andorra, that bottle-cap-size country that sits high in the Pyrenees, stranded between France and Spain like a backpack that someone lost on a hiking trip and never went back to retrieve. Most promising of all, he's here to visit his great friend Alfredo Ayala. Ayala is Puerto Rican, well-connected, not quite skinny. Ripert met him in 1986 when they were both working at Joël Robuchon's late Paris restaurant Jamin; Ayala invited Ripert home to Puerto Rico for a visit. Ripert took him up on it almost immediately, showing up on his next vacation with his latest girlfriend. Over the years there were many vacations and at least as many girlfriends, until the day when Ripert got off the plane with a woman and Ayala said, "Eric, you're going to marry this one."

Ayala slips his Jaguar into the stream of taillights pouring into Old San Juan. "It's so good to be back in Puerto Rico," Ripert says, as we slide past the ruins of a Spanish fort with two photographers, a painter and a writer to put together a chapter for his book, *A Return to Cooking.* "You spend a week here and you come back feeling...strong!" He punctuates this with a raised fist.

In the morning, Ayala will drive us to the El Yunque rain forest, where he keeps a restaurant, and the day after that he and Ripert will cook a Puerto Rican feast. But tonight he's going to take us around the old colonial quarter of San Juan for dinner at Aguaviva, where a cosmopolitan crowd dines on shellfish platters and Nuevo Latino seafood under cool blue lights that give the whole place a coral-reef feel. Some friends of Ripert's show up, and then some friends of theirs, and pretty soon we have taken over a whole corner of the dining room. One waiter seems to take it as his sacred duty to refill our wineglasses; another, tipped off that a celebrity chef is in the house, brings us everything on the left side of the menu, starting with a mussel seviche, and then moves to the right side, with a couscous-based paella, ignoring our

"Spend a week here and you come back feeling strong."

ERIC RIPERT

The lovely beaches outside San Juan.

pleas to stop. Then somebody mentions that there's a salsa festival in town all week, with bands and dancers from around the world.

"I've been coming to Puerto Rico 16 years and I've never learned to dance salsa," Ripert says with a long face. "Can you believe?"

A girl at the end of the table offers to teach Ripert to dance if he'll show her how to cook. He looks doubtful, but in a few minutes we are speeding back toward the Hilton, where the night's big salsa event is underway. We breeze past the doorman. Ayala buys a round of Cuba Libres. An all-female Colombian combo is on the stage, spellbinding in blue-sequined halter tops and matching hip-huggers. There are 12 of them, or maybe 13. I keep counting, and keep losing track. They won't hold still. Unbelievable things are happening on the dance floor. The people here seem to have evolved extra joints that allow their hips to move in ways unknown off this island. We watch a girl with a 12-inch waist and Crystal Gayle's hair shimmy with an intense bald man whose white shirt is unbuttoned down to the equator. They look like they've been dancing together at least 40 years, which would be several times longer than she's been alive. Ripert tries to make like the locals, but it's hopeless.

A bit too early the next day, Ripert and Ayala pick me up for a trip to a market in the Santurce district, southeast of Old San Juan. Ripert's first stop is a botanica selling the magic candles, herbs and other items with which Puerto Ricans supplement their Catholicism. "I always come here to get candles," Ripert says. "For protection. My wife thinks I'm crazy. Of course, I am." The market is Sunday-morning sleepy, with a handful of laconic vendors adjusting their displays of tubers in endless varieties and plantains of outstanding girth. Ripert and Ayala pick out some fruits and coconuts for later use, squeezing and pinching and shaking.

After loading our groceries into the trunk, we start the two-hour drive to Ayala's restaurant. Actually, there's a multilane highway that will get you there in about 45 minutes, but the multilane highway doesn't go through Piñones. When I dreamed of plantains bubbling happily in hot fat, I was imagining someplace very much like Piñones. The map indicates a town, but Piñones is really not much more than a turnoff on Route 187 where a dozen or so Chiclets-colored shacks provide fried snacks for motorists on their way to or from the beach. The culinary technology at Piñones must look paleolithic to Ripert. It would look paleolithic to a sidewalk hot-dog vendor. Massive pots of oil, shellacked to a profound blackness by seasons of smoke and burnt grease, sit above burning slats of wood that seem to have been salvaged from the wreckage of the last hurricane. The cooks—most of them women—roll mounds of batter into fritters using a sea-grape leaf. When the fritters have the burnished hue of an old saddle, they're threaded onto coat-hanger wires or car-radio antennas to drip and cool.

Those fritters: First, the *bacalaito,* a deep-fried pancake of salt cod, garlic, oregano, flour and water. Then, the *alcapurria,* a long, deep-fried torpedo of grated arrowroot or yuca filled with ground beef or crabmeat. Finally, the signal achievement of Piñones, possibly the form to

With chef Alfredo Ayala at the wheel, Ripert checks out roadside *tostones*—smashed, fried plantains—which he'll pair with smoked salmon. Later, Ripert and writer Pete Wells relax over cocktails.

CALLE
DE
SAN SEBA

which all fried foods aspire, the *pionono*. A sweet plantain is wrapped around a handful of ground beef or crab, then covered with a simple egg batter that holds the whole package together as it fries.

All the shacks have the same menu. Ripert prefers one called El Piñonero, although it's distinguishable from Mi Sitio and Melody and El 24 de Diciembre only by its color, which is blue.

"Did you try the *alcapurria de jueyes,* with crabmeat?" he asks, holding one out to me. "It's fantastic, right?" Then, mixing his messages, he says, "Don't eat everything. We are going to another shack. It's much more typical. This one is almost too sophisticated. Where we're going, it might not even be there anymore. It was there in January, but if there was a strong wind last week..." He trails off, leaving me to picture fritters blowing down the highway like tumbleweeds.

Luckily, El Primero y El Último is sturdier than it looks. You wouldn't call it sophisticated—while we place our orders, a pregnant mongrel noses around our feet—but the cooking here has a layer of refinement that sets it apart from El Piñonero, if the definition of refinement can accommodate a deep-fried torpedo. Still, we are centuries away from the checkerboards of raw fish Ripert assembles back home.

"The meal I am going to make tomorrow, it won't be fancy, because Puerto Rico is not about fanciness," he says. "It's about strength. It's about power."

We buy green coconuts for the road and stand back as their lids are lopped off with a machete. Coconut water, drunk straight from the shell through a straw, is said to settle the stomach, making it a wise insurance policy on this day of fritter hunting.

Ripert notices everything on the roadside, from the blindingly white egrets standing frozen in the grass to the stooped old man loading his red wheelbarrow with fallen coconuts. As we begin to climb away from the coast and into the mountains of the El Yunque rain forest, he calls out, "Look how thick those bamboos are! That tree there—red and yellow and orange and green all together! That's God being creative." We pass a strip of gas stations. "And that's us being creative. Hmm. We have some work to do before we catch up."

A monk parakeet swoops low over the car as we pull up beside Ayala's restaurant, Las Vegas. Ayala bought the place in 2000 and gave it a clean, modern look and tropical-fruit colors. Ask him how it looked before the renovation and he closes his eyes and shudders expressively. He didn't think much of the name Las Vegas, either, but he kept it out of respect for the families who'd been eating there for years. Instantly, Ayala and Ripert head to the bar to construct a rum punch: oranges, limes, sugar, Puerto Rican rum. The surprises—and a rum punch needs to have some tricks up its sleeve to surprise me—are basil leaves and Thai chile peppers. Poured over crushed ice, with a topping of nutmeg, it's hot and cold and sweet and sour and just exactly what we need to take the teeth out of the afternoon heat.

Dinner at Las Vegas is my first hint of what Ripert and Ayala are plotting for tomorrow. The food is lovingly faithful to the spirit of Puerto Rico, yet Ayala's training abroad betrays itself in the way the flavors have been sharpened and focused. An appetizer of dorade skewered

On the way to Ayala's restaurant, Ripert makes a detour to the best snack shacks to try fritters of all kinds.

between squares of bacon brings Ripert to a dead halt. "This is very good," he says, popping another chunk of grilled fish into his mouth. "It's *very* good. Alfredo, what is the sauce?" Ayala gives up his secret: a passion fruit reduction with whole-grain mustard, one of those two-ingredient miracles that are only possible from a chef who knows when to stop. And now it is time to stop. Tomorrow holds a full day of cooking, and eating, and the chefs need their sleep.

When I meet up with Ayala and Ripert at a friend's house the next morning, the temperature is already in the 90s; the humidity is near the saturation point. The 800,000 Puerto Ricans living in New York City may be the only people in history to have moved there for the weather. Ripert is bowed over the stove, wearing shorts and a gold chain. That's it. "Forget the Naked Chef," he says. "Here's the real naked chef!"

Stockpots are blowing more steam into the air, if that's possible. Ripert is browning chicken for his coconut coq au vin. "There is nothing more French than a coq au vin," he says. "And

TRAVEL TIPS

WHERE TO STAY

• HOTEL EL CONVENTO Overlooking the bay in the middle of Old San Juan, the 58-room Hotel El Convento is a colonial beauty. Bedrooms have marble chessboard or terra-cotta tile floors and wooden shutters. The hotel started life in 1651 as a convent, then did less salubrious stints as dance hall, flophouse and garage (100 Cristo St.; 800-468-2779; doubles $195 to $450; www.elconvento.com).

• THE GALLERY INN New York–born watercolor artist Jan D'Esopo displays her work throughout this 18th-century Spanish colonial house in Old San Juan. The 22 adorable, air-conditioned guest rooms, most opening onto gardens and patios or with private terraces, are adorned with trompe l'oeil murals and antique furniture (Calle Norzagaray 204–206; 787-722-1808; doubles $145 to $350; www.thegalleryinn.com).

WHERE TO EAT

• AGUAVIVA A happening restaurant in Old San Juan serving Nuevo Latino seafood dishes such as mussel seviche (364 Calle Fortaleza; 787-722-0665).

• LAS VEGAS At his restaurant in the El Yunque rain forest, chef Alfredo Ayala treats Puerto Rican ingredients with respect and imagination. The grilled dorade skewers are a standout (Road 191, Km 1.3, Rio Grande; 787-887-2526).

then to add coconut milk to that! My God! That is pure Puerto Rican inspiration." His tenure in France peeks through everywhere; he's skimming, degreasing and tasting all the time, scooping away some of the chorizo broth in which he'll simmer the red beans, adding fresh water to dilute the salt. His assistant, Andrea Glick, is doing what chefs' assistants do: slicing garlic, chopping parsley and blithely ignoring Ripert's hints that she's doing it all wrong.

Ayala, for his part, is stewing pigeon peas with some herbs from the yard. Satisfied with his progress, he leads me along a serpentine path through the garden on a quick botanical tour. The jungle has a hyperactive imagination. Every plant is pushing out a flower or a fruit, and each one represents a completely new idea of what a flower or fruit should look like. At our approach, bright green lizards make superhero leaps onto the nearest banana leaf. As Ayala stands on the patio, pointing out the course of a small stream that cascades down a ravine to the ocean, a ripe breadfruit crashes to the concrete with a meaty slap familiar to devotees of the boxing ring.

From inside, I hear Ripert calling, *"El lechón! El lechón!"* He emerges onto the patio, trailed by a man carrying a roast suckling pig. I'm pretty sure it's the same pig that had been rolling above the charcoal pit of my dreams back at the Hilton.

"Is that part of your menu?" I ask.

"No, it's for us to snack on before the guests get here," Ripert says. Then he tears off a crisp, golden ear and starts to chew. And chew.

The guests are late—bad news for the structural integrity of the suckling pig but good news for the chef, as the coq au vin is taking forever to get tender. "That's because it's a real chicken," Ripert says, "not one of those stupid birds we get at home that cook in five minutes."

And it gives him time to split the gambas—a kind of shrimp—so that by the time two cars pull into the driveway, he's ready to light the grill. The shrimp cook in just about the time it takes Ripert to brush them with shallot butter. A squeeze of lime, then an incendiary shot of rum, and they're ready for their trip to the buffet table, already loaded with coq au vin, pigeon peas, red beans, white rice and smoked salmon on fried green plantains.

It rains a lot in the rain forest (hence the name), but today the humidity can't seem to find the energy to organize itself into drops. One of Ripert's guests, a man he describes as "the godfather of the island," has brought cigars. Ripert pulls on one, sending plumes of smoke into the jungle. He's been cooking for seven hours now, and the heat is finally catching up with him. Luckily, dessert has just four ingredients—bananas, lime juice, sugar and eggs—which will come together in a soufflé that, in this climate, may actually be lighter than air.

Finally, there's nothing left to cook and nothing left to eat. Ripert suggests that we all drive up the mountain for a swim. "There's a waterfall up the road. You stand under it and you just feel so..."

You can have your well-fed local guides. Me, I'm sticking with the skinny French guy.

BY PETE WELLS

In El Yunque, Ripert creates
Latin-accented recipes.

Ripert's fried plantain chips were inspired by food from the roadside fritter stalls.

Chorizo and Pinto-Bean Stew

4 SERVINGS

½ pound dried pinto beans, soaked overnight and drained (1½ cups)

3 cups chicken stock or low-sodium broth

¼ pound sweet chorizo

¼ pound hot chorizo

¼ cup Classic Sofrito (recipe follows)

One 2-ounce piece of smoked ham

1 medium tomato, seeded and coarsely chopped

1 small carrot, halved

1 small celery rib, halved

1 small onion, quartered

1 parsley sprig

1 oregano sprig

Salt and freshly ground pepper

Lime wedges, for serving

1. In a medium saucepan, combine the beans with the stock, chorizos, Classic Sofrito, ham, tomato, carrot, celery, onion, parsley and oregano and bring to a boil. Simmer over low heat, skimming occasionally, until the beans are tender, about 1½ hours.

2. Remove the chorizos; slice them ¼ inch thick and return to the stew. Remove the carrot, coarsely chop it and return to the stew. Discard the parsley and oregano and season the stew with salt and pepper. Serve the bean stew with the lime wedges.

MAKE AHEAD The stew can be refrigerated for up to 3 days. Reheat gently.

SERVE WITH Steamed rice.

WINE A rustic red with enough fruit and spice will tame the chorizo in this stew. Look for an inexpensive Malbec from Argentina.

Classic Sofrito

MAKES ABOUT 1 CUP

This spicy, garlicky condiment from Eric Ripert's old friend Alfredo Ayala is excellent with all kinds of bean stews as well as with scrambled eggs, quesadillas or grilled meats.

3 garlic cloves

Kosher salt

2 tablespoons extra-virgin olive oil

1 medium white onion, finely chopped

2 or 3 Scotch bonnet chiles, with some seeds, finely chopped

1 medium tomato—peeled, seeded and coarsely chopped

¼ cup coarsely chopped cilantro leaves

On a cutting board, mince the garlic, then mash it with a large pinch of salt. Heat the olive oil in a medium saucepan. Add the onion and chiles and cook over low heat until softened, about 5 minutes. Add the mashed garlic and cook, stirring, for 1 minute. Add the tomato and cook over moderately high heat until the juices have evaporated, about 4 minutes. Stir in the chopped cilantro and let cool.

MAKE AHEAD The cooked sofrito can be refrigerated for up to 3 days.

Grilled Jumbo Shrimp with Garlic-Herb Butter

4 FIRST-COURSE SERVINGS

The best way to eat these shrimp in the shell is to peel them at the table and lick the garlicky butter off your fingers.

1 stick (4 ounces) unsalted butter

¼ cup finely chopped parsley

¼ cup finely chopped basil

3 garlic cloves, finely chopped

1 shallot, finely chopped

16 jumbo shrimp in their shell, preferably with their heads left on, rinsed and patted dry

Salt and freshly ground pepper

White rum, for sprinkling (optional)

Celebrating the food and the drinks of Puerto Rico.

1. In a small saucepan, combine the butter with the chopped parsley, basil, garlic and shallot and melt over low heat.

2. Light a grill or heat a grill pan. Halve the shrimp lengthwise, leaving them attached 1 inch below the head. Devein the shrimp and spread them open. Season with salt and pepper, then brush liberally with the herb butter.

3. Grill the shrimp over a medium-hot fire, shell side down, until lightly charred, about 1 minute. Turn and grill the other side until lightly browned, about 40 seconds. Turn the shrimp again. Brush them liberally with more herb butter, sprinkle with rum and grill until barely cooked through and bubbling, about 1 minute longer. Serve at once.

MAKE AHEAD The garlic-herb butter can be refrigerated overnight in an airtight container. Melt the butter before using.

WINE An aromatic, soft, spicy white, such as a Pinot Gris from Argentina, will contrast with the pungent garlic and smoky grilled flavors.

Tostones with Smoked Salmon

4 HORS D'OEUVRE SERVINGS

Tostones—fried, smashed plantain slices— are a great variation on the toast used for the hors d'oeuvre of smoked salmon and

herbed cream. Soaking the plantain slices may seem like an unnecessary step, but it helps remove some of their starchiness and keeps them white.

> 2 **large green plantains (about 10 ounces each)**
>
> 6 **cups water**
>
> **Kosher salt**
>
> 2 **cups vegetable oil, for frying the plantains**
>
> ⅓ **cup sour cream**
>
> 2 **tablespoons very finely chopped dill, plus several dill sprigs for garnish**
>
> 2 **teaspoons fresh lime juice**
>
> 6 **ounces thinly sliced cold-smoked salmon, cut into 12 uniform pieces**
>
> 1 **large lime, quartered then sliced paper-thin, for garnish**

1. Cut off both ends of the green plantains and score them lengthwise, then peel off the skin. In a large bowl, combine the water with 1 teaspoon of kosher salt. Add the peeled plantains and let them soak for 30 minutes. Drain the plantains and pat them dry with paper towels. Cut each plantain on the diagonal into 6 slices, each one about 1½ inches thick.

2. In a large skillet, heat the oil to 275°. Add the plantain slices and fry, stirring frequently, for 2 minutes. Transfer the plantain slices to paper towels to drain and let cool slightly. Reserve the oil in the skillet.

3. Wrap each plantain slice in a dampened paper towel and use a meat pounder to gently pound it into a ¼-inch-thick oval.

4. In a small bowl, using a spoon, stir the sour cream with the chopped dill and fresh lime juice until thoroughly combined.

5. Reheat the oil to 375°. Add the flattened plantains and fry, turning once, until golden and crisp, about 2 minutes. Drain the *tostones* on paper towels, then sprinkle with salt.

6. Dollop 1½ teaspoons of the herbed sour cream on each *tostone*. Top each *tostone* with a slice of smoked salmon, garnish with a dill sprig and lime slice. Repeat with the remaining *tostones*, salmon, dill and lime and serve.

MAKE AHEAD The recipe can be prepared through Step 4 up to 4 hours in advance. Refrigerate the herbed sour cream, but keep the plantains at room temperature.

WINE The crisp acidity and fresh citrus fruit of an American nonvintage brut sparkling wine, make it a natural foil for the rich smoked salmon and herbed cream.

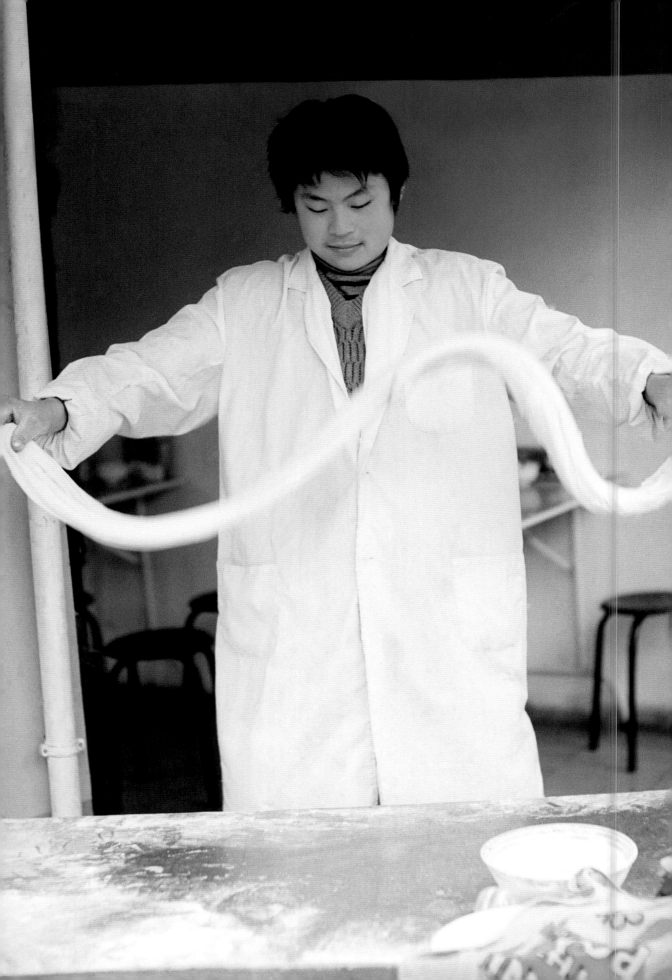

JEAN-GEORGES VONGERICHTEN
Shanghai

Jean-Georges Vongerichten of New York's Jean Georges recently opened the very French Jean Georges Shanghai, LEFT. Meanwhile, Shanghai specialties, like noodles, OPPOSITE, inspired him to open 66 in Manhattan.

Sometimes I think I can get inside Jean-Georges Vongerichten's head. After working as his editor at FOOD & WINE, I understand how he grafts Asian flavors onto French techniques at both Jean Georges in New York and Vong, which has outposts in Hong Kong, Chicago and Manhattan. But now, after a few trips to Shanghai, he's started bringing French ingredients into Asian dishes. In February 2003, he opened the Chinese restaurant 66 in Manhattan, where he tucks foie gras into *hargow* (shrimp dumplings) and blends fresh water chestnuts with an ethereal shellfish mousse to create a shrimp toast that wouldn't be out of place at a Michelin-starred establishment. He also opened JG, a high-end French restaurant, in Shanghai in April 2004. What was so special about Shanghai, I wondered, that it could convince Vongerichten to launch not one but two new projects?

When I went to ask Vongerichten this question at sleek, minimalist 66, he was having his picture taken for a French magazine. He stood in front of the Richard Meier–designed fish tanks flanked by several giggling twentysomething hostesses in slim Vivienne Tam pants. Another photographer, who had the next appointment with him, sat at one of the

A trip to Shanghai is the answer to understanding Asian flavors.

Vongerichten transforms Shanghai street food, OPPOSITE, into his **Stir-Fried Noodles with Roast Pork.**

white Eero Saarinen tables in the lounge, having long finished her ginger margarita.

While I waited my turn, I perched on a stool at the 40-seat communal table and tried to eat my way to an understanding of Vongerichten's latest endeavor. Instead, the dishes just raised new questions. Was the lacquered pork with a shallot-and-ginger confit that tasted like a jammy sauerkraut a nod to his roots in Alsace? What was tuna tartare doing on a Chinese menu? The seafood—the lobster claw steamed with ginger and Shaoxing wine, say, or the two-flavored shrimp, one half in a sweet-and-sour sauce and the other in a mayonnaise-like condensed-milk mixture—was so fresh and perfectly prepared that I wanted to send the entire F&W staff to the restaurant for a cooking lesson. Is shellfish important in Shanghai, too?

I barraged Vongerichten with these questions, but he only had one response: "You have to go to Shanghai," he said again and again. "You will understand when you go."

On my first day in Shanghai, Handel Lee, the 44-year-old Chinese American developer of the Three on the Bund project, where Vongerichten's restaurant is located, had a car and driver waiting for me at my hotel. I'm used to walking everywhere, or at least taking public transportation, to get the feel for a city. But I was staying at the Grand Hyatt Shanghai in the Jin Mao Tower in Pudong, the new financial center across the Huangpu River from downtown Shanghai, and, as we circled the tower, the world's fourth-tallest building, then ducked into a tunnel and merged onto elevated highways, I realized how sprawling the city is. Shanghai has an efficient new subway system, but everything is so far away from everything else that after a few days, I was grateful that the taxis are so inexpensive and the drivers so agreeable, especially since few of them speak English.

Some of my first impressions were as I expected: We passed alleyways crisscrossed by washing on clotheslines and people of all ages practicing tai chi in parks and along the roads. But the city was also far more cosmopolitan than I'd thought. Shanghai is the largest city in China, I soon learned, with about 20 million people. Among them are tens of thousands of foreigners—Japanese, Koreans, Europeans and Americans. And to judge from the billboards advertising everything from Louis Vuitton and KFC to the Thai-owned Lotus supermarkets and Andrew Lloyd Webber's *Cats* at the Shanghai Grand Theatre, they're all here to do business.

That's what Handel Lee's role is: to help Westerners like Vongerichten set up shop. Hundreds of companies of the Fortune 500 are represented in Shanghai today, and the city has attracted foreign entrepreneurs for centuries. By the early 1900s, the most important international banks, shipping lines and trading houses all had addresses on the Bund, a mile-long embankment of grandiose Western-style stone mansions along the Huangpu River. Despite the frantic rush over the past decade to bulldoze old Shanghai and replace it with skyscrapers, the Bund hasn't been touched. "The Bund is sacred ground for Shanghai,"

Old Shanghai, with its traditional foods, street vendors and alleyways crisscrossed by clothes-lines, exists side by side with new Shanghai, with its stylish shoppers and Western-style restaurants.

Bass with caramelized onions and steamed dumplings. OPPOSITE: **Asparagus soup with lemony dumplings.**

Lee said. "The government is obsessed with making sure it's developed right."

Lee took me on a hard-hat tour of Three on the Bund, a seven-story building with a baroque turret, Gothic arched windows and a Romanesque tympanum erected in 1916. Though the exterior of the building remained as is, the postmodernist American architect Michael Graves transformed the interior, designing an atrium surrounded by an Evian day spa, Vongerichten's restaurant, the Shanghai Gallery of Arts, a Chinese restaurant called the Whampoa Club and one of Nobu Matsuhisa's restaurants. Vongerichten must have realized that his modern French food would appeal to the same international, affluent customer who'd want Chinese art and French beauty treatments in the same building.

went to Bao Luo first because it was Vongerichten's favorite restaurant in Shanghai. A bicycle repairman started Bao Luo with a few tables; it now holds 300 people in a tight warren of rooms. Polished granite is everywhere—on the floor and the walls—and even the lamp shades are made of stone. That may sound opulent, but in Shanghai the entrance to every hotel, office building, supermarket and subway seems to be made out of granite. There's no coat check; instead, you fling your coat over the back of your chair and someone covers it with green plastic stamped with the name of the restaurant. Groups of Chinese office workers crowd around tables, digging into mostly classic Shanghai dishes: wok-fried snake, eels and braised turtle. Something called Swiss steak—spicy beef barbecued with a mayonnaise sauce—is also popular.

Although the food was recognizably Chinese, I had never seen most of the dishes before. The cuisine of eastern China, including Shanghai, tends to be slightly sweeter than Cantonese cooking and less spicy than Sichuan. Because the city is located on the Yangtze River delta, the Shanghainese eat lots of freshwater fish and shellfish—river shrimp, crabs, frog's legs, turtles and eels.

Bao Luo's menu, which includes English translations, is as thick as a manual on how to build your own harpsichord, and about as useful. Like most places in Shanghai, the restaurant features a long list of cold marinated dishes, including smoked fish, bean-curd skin,

For his restaurant Jean Georges Shanghai, Vongerichten snagged a 1916 building on the Bund, along the Huangpu River, one of Asia's most famous cityscapes.

The stone mansions along the Bund are sacred in Shanghai.

jellyfish, salted chicken and drunken crab—raw crab marinated in a mixture of rice wine, soy sauce, ginger and spring onions. You pick out the bits of shell and cartilage with chopsticks to get at the creamy roe and sweet flesh. All the vegetables are good, especially the stir-fried grass heads, a wild spring green. Nobody seems to order white rice, but the Shanghainese are especially fond of soup. Whenever I didn't order it, my waiter was sure to mention that I'd forgotten my soup and ask which one I wanted.

I knew one dish I had to taste at Bao Luo: a sweet-and-sour fish that inspired Vongerichten at 66. At Bao Luo the recipe is unrefined: The fish is deep-fried whole in a heavy batter and set in a thick sauce showered with carrots, peas and pine nuts. Vongerichten transforms the dish: He dips one side of a black bass fillet in a cake-flour-and-baking-powder slurry that fries up to a light, crisp crust. He tucks the pine nuts under the fillet and lightens and sharpens the sauce. Vongerichten saw the possibility in a dish that I would have otherwise dismissed.

Just down the street from Bao Luo, I found Guyi Hunan, a place that shows just how broad-minded the Shanghainese have become. A few years ago a chile-laden dish would have been unusual in Shanghai, but now fusion, Italian, Thai, Indian and fiery Hunan restaurants like Guyi Hunan are commonplace. The crowd in the room, decorated with black-and-white photographs of old Shanghai, is stylish and young—one Chinese guy had blond hair, another was using a cigarette holder. No one was wearing a suit. Hunan food is known to numb the taste buds with chiles—and indeed the pork ribs with chiles and cumin were incredibly tender and spicy. But not all the dishes at Guyi Hunan were wildly hot. The cold braised kabocha squash with lily bulbs, which have the texture of onion but not the pungency, was fresh and aromatic.

The next morning I joined Jereme Leung, who is the executive chef at the Whampoa Club at Three on the Bund, for breakfast at his favorite dumpling spot, Wang Jia Sha. Vongerichten has several versions of *xiao long bao,* Shanghai's famous soup dumplings, on his menu at 66, and Leung, who had spent six years as a dim sum chef, promised me this state-owned place served a classic.

Located on Nanjing Road, Shanghai's neon-lit shopping street, Wang Jia Sha, with its formica tables bolted to the linoleum floor, is the Chinese version of the Howard Johnson's in New York City's Times Square. White-capped ladies sit in the front window rolling out dough and pinching it around a pork or crab filling, both of which are enriched with bits of lard—the Shanghainese aren't afraid of fat. While Leung went to the counter to order, I slid into a yellow plastic chair downstairs. (Prices are three times higher on the second floor, which has waiter service.)

The soup dumplings at Wang Jia Sha are so juicy that you have to learn how to eat them or risk a dry-cleaning disaster. Leung demonstrated: First, dip a dumpling in black rice vinegar, which was set on every table in a teapot, and place it on a soupspoon to catch

Boots are essential in Shanghai's wet markets.

In Pudong, old-fashioned shops selling all kinds of skewers set off the Grand Hyatt Shanghai, with its soaring atrium.

the broth. Take a tiny bite out of one side and suck out the hot liquid. Then eat the rest as quickly as you can. "Temperature is important with Chinese food," Leung explained. "Three or four minutes changes everything."

One of Vongerichten's aims at 66 is to turn out food that is fresher and lighter than the original Chinese. His crab dumplings, for instance, have flakes of crab instead of crab paste, a cleaner flavor and a serious hit of ginger. After tasting the delicious high-fat version at Wang Jia Sha, I decide that in fiddling with the meat-to-fat ratio, Vongerichten hasn't really improved on the original. He's just created an entirely different dumpling.

Wandering over to Wujiang Road, a pedestrian street lined with restaurants and snack stalls off of Nanjing West Road, I wound up having a second breakfast. The brick street's two-story buildings are a piece of old Shanghai, though I could see the skyscrapers looming behind them. The road is just a few blocks long, but the peddlers sell every conceivable kind of street food: skewers of quail and tripe, chicken feet, puffy steamed buns, chow mein with shredded baby cabbage and carrots, *zifan* (shredded pork and salted mustard greens in a roll of glutinous rice) and *jian bing* (a fried cruller wrapped in a crêpe).

At Xiao Yang Shengjian, the house specialty is *sheng jian bao,* pork-filled dumplings that are steamed, then fried, so they're crunchy on the bottom; sesame seeds and scallions are sprinkled on top. Four dumplings cost $2, and diners can take the chipped white enamelware plates to one of the communal tables on the street or inside the restaurant. The chopsticks are wooden and stained with black vinegar, and you tear off toilet paper to use as a napkin, but this is dumpling heaven.

An outdoor pedestrian mall, Xintiandi is also a preserved bit of Shanghai, but it's far more upscale than Wujiang Road—it could be the template for Three on the Bund. Xintiandi escaped the wrecker's ball partly because Shui On, its Hong Kong developer, promised to restore the house where the Communist party was founded—paradoxical, since the new restaurants and stores are all privately owned, while previous regimes required that the state own all businesses. In the gray brick-and-stone 19th-century houses, there are art galleries, fashion boutiques, nightclubs, *pâtisseries,* a German brew pub, a place called Cheese & Fizz that sells French wines and the cheeses of French master ager Bernard Antony, and a dozen restaurants. One of the most popular is the Shanghai-style restaurant Xinjishi, which serves a delicious braised pork with brown sauce—equal parts meat and fat—and sweet, warm Chinese dates (small, wrinkled fruit that look like red olives) stuffed with glutinous rice.

Soahc, one of Xintiandi's restaurants, is a typically stylish tenant. Owner Lily Ho, a former Hong Kong movie star, placed a carp-filled pond at the entrance, so patrons literally cross a bridge to leave the city's noise and crowds behind. Inside, the two floors of dining rooms have high ceilings with polished dark wood beams and oversize booths. Silver-edged ebony chopsticks lie on elegant rests shaped like shiitake mushrooms.

Shanghai's famous shopping
street, Nanjing Road.

The cooking at Soahc is Yangzhou style, a refined cousin of the Shanghai style. Yangzhou, a city north of Shanghai, is famous for foods cut with geometrical precision, so the cold appetizers are spectacularly presented: curls of marinated lotus root filled with pureed longan; braised pig's trotters formed into a terrine and served sliced with sweet vinegar sauce; delicate fans of crispy *wo ju,* which tastes similar to cucumber. If a businessman needs to impress a client with obvious symbols of extravagance, he can find plenty of dishes with shark fin and abalone, the Chinese equivalent of foie gras and truffles. But my favorite dish here, a soup, is distinctly less elevated: Yangzhou-style pressed bean curd, fine strands the width of vermicelli, served in chicken broth with julienned ginger and tiny heads of baby bok choy along with sweet river shrimp.

When I ate at 66 after I got back from Shanghai, I saw everything in a different way. I observed that 66 could fit easily into the mix of restaurants in Xintiandi. The family-style service seemed normal, too, after Shanghai. How odd it would feel to eat this food in courses and to share a table with fewer than six people. I'd found so many different kinds of cuisines on my trip—sometimes at the same restaurant—that the blending of Shanghai, Cantonese, Thai and French at 66 now seemed to reflect modern Shanghai. This time when I ate the lacquered pork belly, it reminded me of China, not France: It was braised in a soy-sauce marinade, just like at Xinjishi. And I understood that the tuna tartare was an homage to the raw drunken crab.

When Vongerichten stopped by my table to ask if I had any questions, I realized the trip to Shanghai had given me all the answers.

BY JANE SIGAL

TRAVEL TIPS

WHERE TO STAY
- GRAND HYATT SHANGHAI in Mao Tower; 800-633-7313.
- ST. REGIS SHANGHAI, 889 Dongfang Rd.; 877-787-3447.

WHERE TO EAT
- BAO LUO, 271 Fumin Rd.; 011-86-21-6279-2827. • GUYI HUNAN, 89 Fumin Rd.; 011-86-21-6249-5628.
- SOAHC, NO. 3, 123 Xing Ye Rd.; 011-86-21-6385-7777. • WANG JIA SHA, 805 Nanjing Rd.; 011-86-21-6253-0404. • XIAO YANG SHENGJIAN, 54 Wujiang Rd.; no telephone. • XINJISHI, No. 2, 181 Long Tai Cang Rd.; 011-86-21-3307-0761.

Shanghai's street food is unfamiliar yet irresistible.

Stir-Fried Chinese Noodles with Roast Pork

4 SERVINGS

Jean-Georges Vongerichten thinks the best food in Asia can be found at street stalls. In the early mornings, Shanghai vendors with gas-powered woks stir-fry dishes like these simple egg noodles.

- 1 **pound thin Chinese yellow or egg noodles**
- ½ **cup chicken stock or low-sodium broth**
- 2 **tablespoons oyster sauce**
- 2 **tablespoons soy sauce**
- 2 **teaspoons sugar**
- ¼ **teaspoon chili oil**

Kosher salt

- 2 **tablespoons vegetable oil**
- 2 **large eggs, lightly beaten**
- 1 **large carrot, julienned**
- 1 **large celery rib, julienned**
- ½ **pound Chinese roast pork, cut into thin strips**
- 1 **scallion, white and green parts, thinly sliced**

1. Bring a large saucepan of water to a boil. Add the noodles and cook them, stirring occasionally, until al dente, about 3 minutes. Drain in a colander and return the noodles to the pan. Fill the pan with cold water, swish the noodles and drain; repeat. Leave the noodles in the colander and lift them with your fingers occasionally to dry slightly.

2. In a small bowl, blend the stock with the oyster sauce, soy sauce, sugar, chili oil and 1 teaspoon of salt.

3. Heat 1 tablespoon of the vegetable oil in a wok. Add the eggs and cook over moderate heat, stirring, until set, about 1 minute. Trans-

fer the eggs to a plate and break them up into small chunks. Add the remaining 1 tablespoon of vegetable oil to the wok and heat until shimmering. Add the carrot and celery and stir-fry over moderately high heat until softened, about 3 minutes. Add the pork, noodles and sauce mixture and toss to coat. Season lightly with salt, add the scallion and eggs and toss well. Transfer to a large, shallow bowl and serve at once.

BEER A bright, refreshing lager with some sweet hoppy flavor will complement the rich roast pork and oyster sauce. Go for an Asian lager, such as Tiger Beer from Singapore or Singha from Thailand.

Creamy Asparagus Soup with Lemon Dumplings

6 SERVINGS

Vongerichten's new restaurant in Shanghai is French, but with updated dishes like this. "Even classic French restaurants have evolved," he says.

- 4 **tablespoons unsalted butter**
- 1 **tablespoon extra-virgin olive oil**
- 2 **large shallots, thinly sliced (1½ cups)**
- 2 **pounds medium asparagus, 1½-inch tips reserved, spears coarsely chopped**

Salt and freshly ground pepper

- 1 **quart chicken stock or low-sodium broth**
- 1 **cup heavy cream**
- 24 **Lemon Dumplings (recipe follows)**

1. In a large saucepan, melt 2 tablespoons of the butter in the olive oil. Add the shallots and cook over low heat until softened, about

5 minutes. Add the chopped asparagus, season with salt and pepper and cook, stirring, until softened, about 5 minutes. Add the chicken stock and cream and bring to a boil over moderately high heat. Reduce the heat to moderately low and simmer until the asparagus is very tender, about 15 minutes.

2. Meanwhile, bring a medium saucepan of water to a boil. Add salt and the asparagus tips and cook until just tender, about 3 minutes. Using a slotted spoon, remove the tips and reserve them; keep the water boiling.

3. Puree the soup in batches in a food processor and strain it through a coarse sieve, pressing on the solids. Return the soup to the large saucepan, season with salt and pepper and add the asparagus tips. Keep hot.

4. Add the Lemon Dumplings to the boiling water and cook until just tender, about 1½ minutes; drain. Melt the remaining 2 tablespoons of butter in the same saucepan over moderately high heat. Add the Lemon Dumplings and carefully swirl them in the butter to coat. Add 4 dumplings to each soup plate, ladle the asparagus soup over them and serve at once.

MAKE AHEAD The soup and cooked asparagus tips can be refrigerated for up to 2 days. Reheat gently.

WINE A tart New Zealand Sauvignon Blanc has the acidity and fresh herbal flavor to stand up to the asparagus and lemon in this soup.

Lemon Dumplings

MAKES 2 DOZEN DUMPLINGS

These versions of soup dumplings are filled with a lemon jelly that liquefies when cooked. They would be delicious in a good chicken broth, chicken and rice soup or egg drop soup.

Vongerichten's Crispy Garlic Chicken with Dipping Salt, on the menu at 66, and Spinach with Fried Ginger.

2 large lemons

1 envelope unflavored powdered gelatin

½ tablespoon extra-virgin olive oil

1 teaspoon sugar

Salt

Cayenne pepper

24 square wonton wrappers

1. Finely grate the zest of ½ lemon. Peel all of the lemons, removing the skin and white pith. Working over a large nonreactive saucepan to catch the juice, cut in between the membranes to release the sections. Squeeze the juice from the membranes into the pan. There should be 2 tablespoons of juice. Finely chop the lemon sections and add to the pan. Sprinkle the gelatin over the lemon mixture and let stand until jellied, about 3 minutes.

2. Set the saucepan over low heat and swirl it a few times until the mixture is barely hot and the gelatin has melted, 40 to 50 seconds. Pour the mixture into a shallow glass baking dish, stir in the olive oil and sugar and season with salt and a pinch of cayenne. Refrigerate until very firm, about 2 hours.

3. Scrape the gelatin onto a cutting board and finely chop. Lay 4 wonton wrappers on a work surface and moisten the edges with water. Mound 1 teaspoon of the lemon gelatin just below the center of each wrapper. Bring 2 opposite corners together over the filling to form a triangle. Press all around the filling to release any air pockets and seal the dumplings. Moisten the opposite tips, bring them together and press to seal. Repeat with the remaining wrappers and gelatin.

MAKE AHEAD The dumplings can be frozen for up to a month; cook frozen.

Steamed Buns with Cured Ham

MAKES 16 BUNS

These fluffy buns need two risings. After the second rise, they must be steamed immediately, then they can be held for an hour or two and re-steamed just before serving. Vongerichten's favorite filling for these buns is a dry-cured Smithfield-type ham, which recalls the Yunnan hams found in China.

¾ cup plus 2 tablespoons warm water

2 tablespoons sugar

2 teaspoons active dry yeast

3 cups all-purpose flour

1 tablespoon solid vegetable shortening

2 teaspoons baking powder

Asian sesame oil, for brushing

1 pound sliced ham or Chinese roast pork, or 1½ Chinese roast ducks, sliced crosswise ⅓ inch thick

2 large scallions, julienned

Hoisin sauce (optional)

1. In a small bowl, combine the water with the sugar and yeast; let stand for 5 minutes.

2. Meanwhile, sift the flour into a large bowl. Using a pastry blender, cut in the shortening. Add the baking powder to the yeast mixture, then stir it into the flour. Scrape the dough out onto a work surface and knead until smooth and elastic. Return the dough to the bowl, cover with plastic wrap and let rise until tripled in bulk, about 2 hours.

3. Lightly oil a large baking sheet. Punch down the dough and divide it in half. Cover half of the dough with plastic wrap. Roll the other half into a cylinder about 1 inch in diameter. Cut the cylinder into 8 equal pieces and roll each piece into a ball. Using a rolling pin, roll each ball into a 4-inch round about ⅛ inch thick. Brush the rounds with sesame oil, fold in half and transfer to the baking sheet. Repeat with the remaining dough. Cover the baking sheet loosely with plastic wrap and let the buns rise until doubled in bulk, about 1 hour.

Fish as decoration and sustenance at Bao Luo restaurant, where large groups eat family-style.

4. Generously oil the bottom of a triple-tiered bamboo steamer. Bring 2 inches of water to a boil in a wok. Arrange the buns in the steamer without crowding, set over the boiling water and steam until puffy and cooked, about 5 minutes. Alternatively, oil the basket of a single-layer metal steamer and steam the buns in batches. Immediately transfer the buns to a platter and cover with a tea towel. Serve hot. Let your guests split the buns and fill them with the meat and scallions. Pass the hoisin sauce separately.

Steamed Bass with Caramelized Onion, Ginger and Scallion

2 SERVINGS

Versions of this steamed fish are made all over China, but in Shanghai the recipe always contains a little aged soy sauce. When Vongerichten adapted the dish for 66, he couldn't find aged soy in New York and substituted caramelized onions for sweetness and depth of flavor.

 2 **tablespoons peanut oil**
 1 **small onion, thinly sliced**
Salt
One 1½-inch piece of fresh ginger, peeled and julienned

One 2½-pound whole black sea bass, cleaned and scaled
Soy sauce, for drizzling
 1 **teaspoon Asian sesame oil**
 2 **tablespoons chopped cilantro**
 1 **scallion, cut into 2-inch julienne strips**

1. Heat 1 tablespoon of the peanut oil in a small skillet. Add the onion and a pinch of salt and cook over high heat, stirring once or twice, until browned, about 2 minutes. Transfer to a small bowl and stir in the ginger.

2. In a large wok, set a round rack that will sit at least 3 inches above the bottom. Add 2 inches of water and bring to a boil. Set the fish on a heatproof plate that will fit in the wok and sprinkle the onion and ginger on top. Set the plate on the rack, cover the wok and steam the fish over moderate heat until just cooked through, about 20 minutes.

3. Drizzle the fish with soy sauce. In a small skillet, warm the remaining 1 tablespoon of peanut oil with the sesame oil over moderately high heat, then pour it over the fish. Sprinkle with the cilantro and scallion and serve.

WINE A pure, crisp Riesling Gewürztraminer blend with citrus and spice will balance the salt and complement the fresh ginger.

Spinach with Fried Ginger

6 SERVINGS

 3 **pounds spinach leaves, large stems removed**
One 4-inch piece of fresh ginger, peeled and coarsely chopped (1 cup)
 2 **tablespoons chili oil**
 ½ **cup peanut oil**
 3 **tablespoons soy sauce**
 1 **tablespoon plain rice vinegar**
Large pinch of sugar

1. In a large pot of boiling water, blanch the spinach for barely 1 minute. Drain and rinse well in cold water. Squeeze dry, coarsely chop and transfer to a large, shallow dish.

2. In a mini food processor, finely chop the ginger. Transfer to a small bowl and mix with the chili oil. Let stand for 10 minutes.

3. Heat the peanut oil in a medium skillet. Add the ginger and fry over moderate heat until golden, about 4 minutes. Pour the ginger and oil through a fine sieve and drain the ginger on paper towels.

4. In a small bowl, mix the soy sauce with the vinegar and sugar. Drizzle over the spinach, stir lightly and refrigerate for 20 minutes. Sprinkle the ginger over the spinach and serve.

PINO LUONGO
Tuscany

Chef Pino Luongo of New York City's Coco Pazzo guides cruise-ship guests through fishing villages like Vernazza, LEFT, and Santa Margherita Ligure, CENTER. Villa di Capezzana, OPPOSITE, was once a Medici estate.

The complications of running a cruise ship kitchen are often incompatible with the emphasis in Tuscan cooking on simple seasonality. For instance, when the chef on a Classical Cruise ship wants to order food, he must send a fax to headquarters in Athens, which faxes the local shipping agent, who contacts the chandler in the port of call. When a Tuscan chef like Pino Luongo needs ingredients, however, he goes right to the source, scouring local markets for the best foods and then letting them determine his menu. So a few summers ago, when Luongo led his first weeklong cruise along the coast of Tuscany, it could have been quite a culinary culture clash.

Fortunately, it wasn't. While we made stops on the islands of Elba and Giglio and sailed north to the neighboring region of Liguria, Luongo—a New York City chef and restaurateur who was born and raised in Tuscany—was able to share his philosophy of Tuscan cuisine. He performed cooking demonstrations on the fly, guided impromptu tours of local markets and acted as a genial master of ceremonies at vineyards and restaurants. Luongo made sure the trip accomplished, more or less, what he wanted: to explain a region and its way of life through its food.

The ship was the *Harmony,* a 170-foot yacht with room for 40-odd guests, no bigger, really, than some of the private yachts docked in the Tuscan marinas we visited. Its four

Sandwiches stuffed with a warm salad of squid, mussel and clams.

levels included a kitchen below decks; guest cabins, a dining room and a lounge on the two middle levels; and a large sundeck on top. My cabin was modern and minimalist, with twin beds on either side of a night table and with a smoked-glass door leading to the bathroom. I found the decor spare but elegant, though some guests complained that it was excessively spartan.

We started in Porto Santo Stefano, a town just two hours' drive north of Rome at the southern edge of Tuscany. It is part summer resort, part fishing village; every evening, a fleet of beat-up wooden fishing boats returns with that day's catch. Luongo, a tall, burly, dark-haired man of about 50, grew up just a few miles away. One of his uncles ran a hotel on the edge of town, and another uncle is a retired fisherman who used to raise eels nearby.

While many of the guests slept off their jet lag, Luongo led a small expedition into the port, where rows of fish stalls displayed a wide variety of seafood in long glass cases, from branzino (Mediterranean sea bass) and dentice (similar to snapper) to cuttlefish and clams. "As you can see from the winding, hilly roads around here," Luongo told the group, "it simply doesn't make sense to ship food more than about 30 miles, so people eat what's right around them." Luongo chatted and joked with the fishmongers and, bending normal cruise-line procedure, bought fresh clams, mussels and other seafood for the ship's chef, Lulu Place. That evening she would use them for spaghetti alla pirata, pasta in a light tomato and white wine sauce. Its ingredients vary according to what's available and fresh: Like pirates, you take what you can find.

Luongo is better known as a restaurateur and entrepreneur than as a chef. He owns and runs three restaurants in Manhattan, including Coco Pazzo, Centolire and Tuscan Square. He has found his greatest success helping to popularize Italian cooking that is simple, straightforward and unpretentious: Tellingly, the first of his four cookbooks, *A Tuscan in the Kitchen,* provided ingredient lists but no specific quantities.

Luongo is friendly and personable; he circulated among the cruise guests, many of them loyal regulars at his restaurants, as he might in any of his own dining rooms. He is also plainspoken and makes no bones about having an adversarial relationship with what he calls "the food mafia"—prominent New York food critics whom he regards as clubby and snobbish. Those critics, in turn, have given him a reputation for being difficult.

Over the course of the week, Luongo gave three or four cooking demonstrations on deck. One day, he showed us how to make panzanella, a Tuscan peasant salad of bread, tomatoes and cucumbers dressed in olive oil with scallions, basil and parsley. A volunteer dutifully cut stale, unsalted Tuscan bread into cubes as Luongo fielded questions and expounded his philosophy. Another day he cooked a delicious penne dish that took only about 10 minutes to make, combining high-quality jarred tuna packed in olive oil, capers, parsley and basil. "This is what fishermen around here make for themselves on the boat when they don't have a lot of time or fresh fish to cook with," he explained.

The view from the cruise ship gives a sense of what Tuscan fishermen see every day on the open sea. Another taste of Tuscan life: vegetable panzanella, a salad of bread, tomatoes and cucumbers, which makes the most of humble ingredients.

We all discovered the unpredictability of boat travel when rough seas forced the ship to dock for three days in Portovenere, requiring us to get around by bus, minivan and train. Unfortunately, the local guides the cruise line hired talked constantly. One delivered a monologue about the airports of Italy. Another insisted on identifying the same four or five trees at every curve of the road.

Still, the places themselves were beautiful: the island of Elba, Napoléon's home in exile, with its hills and white sand beaches; the marble mountains of Carrara, whose quarries are visible from the coastal towns, like Forte dei Marmi. Then, as we passed into Liguria, the landscape changed dramatically. Instead of flat sandy beaches with mountains in the distance, the bright green slopes came right down to the water's edge, stark sheer cliffs with luxuriant vegetation growing improbably at about a 60-degree angle. Because of the shortage of flat land on which to build, the port towns on the Italian Riviera have tall, thin houses sometimes six or seven stories high, their bright pastel pinks, oranges, yellows and blues visible far out at sea.

In many ways, visits to two vineyards inland near Florence were the most illuminating part of the trip. Villa di Capezzana at Carmignano, a former Medici estate built in the fourteenth century, has been in the Contini Bonacossi family since 1920. With its marble statues and rose garden, the villa maintains much of its Renaissance grandeur, but it is also very much a working farm, with well-cultivated fields lined with vineyards and olive trees. Among the wines it produces is the highly regarded Super-Tuscan Ghiaie della Furba. The 1998 vintage received the coveted *tre bicchieri* (three glasses) from Italy's leading wine magazine, *Gambero Rosso*.

Beatrice Contini Bonacossi, the owners' daughter, showed us around the estate. The business of food and wine is deeply imbedded in the life of the area, she told us, and not only for those lucky enough to own a villa. Villa di Capezzana, which presses and sells its own olive oil, gives 25 percent of it each year to the local olive pickers. "We prefer to pay them in regular currency," she said, "but they want the olive oil instead." We understood their choice when we got a taste of the oil, which is thick and cloudy green with a distinctive, rich flavor. It is also prized because a tree in Tuscany yields just three liters of oil a year; in southern Italy, a single tree might yield four times as much.

Villa di Capezzana also holds cooking classes, so after the tour, we watched chef Patrizio Cirri prepare risotto with peas from the estate's gardens and pork loin served with an agresto sauce, made with young green grapes. In order to produce top-quality wine, some young grapes are removed from the vines to strengthen the flavor of those that remain. "For many years we just threw these out," Contini Bonacossi explained, "until my mother said, 'Why are we wasting all these grapes?'" The family found an agresto recipe from the Medici period that called for boiling the grapes with onions, garlic, celery, thyme

The steep cliffs of Manarola.

The business
of food and wine
is deeply imbedded
in the life of the area.

Villa di Capezzana, which was built in the
14th century, retains much of its Renaissance
grandeur, but it is also a working farm.

and marjoram. The result has the tanginess of vinegar and the chunky texture of chutney. Initially a family experiment, the agresto is suddenly in commercial demand. "A supplier in the United States wants to know how much we can produce, and at what cost," Contini Bonacossi said. "I have no idea. This is just something my sister made on the stove."

The following day we visited Villa Delia in Ripoli, a beautiful hillside farm about an hour from Florence. Villa Delia was built by Umberto Menghi, a Tuscan chef and restaurateur, who, like Luongo, went to North America to seek his fortune; he now has five successful restaurants in western Canada. Thirteen years ago, Menghi returned to Italy to create a retreat that is part farm, part hotel, part cooking school.

Sitting in a row of chairs before a long, white marble table and a stove, we watched as Menghi and his sister Marietta prepared our lunch of fresh ravioli stuffed with nettle leaves and ricotta. Menghi quickly diced red and yellow peppers ("Don't worry if some of the seeds get into it," he said) and sautéed them with roughly chopped tomato, red onion, carrots, garlic and basil. Then he ran the mixture through a food mill to create a sauce. Marietta made the pasta, cranking the dough through a machine until it was a seven-foot-long sheet. Umberto wrapped it like a scarf around one of the women in our group to show how elastic yet strong it was. "You can put a quail egg in it, you can put fish in it," he explained. "One of the reasons to make pasta at home is to include all the fresh things growing around you."

In that spirit, Luongo stopped at a market that afternoon and found something he had been looking for since we arrived: fava beans. In Porto Santo Stefano, their season was already over because of an unusually warm spring. But here, about a hundred miles north, they were still being harvested. Sitting on deck, we enjoyed a simple bean salad tossed with cubes of *caciotta* cheese, which tastes like a younger, softer version of Pecorino. As Luongo had anticipated, the favas were worth the wait.

BY ALEXANDER STILLE

TRAVEL TIPS

FOOD LOVERS' CRUISES

Pino Luongo hosted this voyage to Italy for Classical Cruises, now Travel Dynamics. For more information on culinary cruises contact TRAVEL DYNAMICS (800-257-5767 or www.traveldynamicsinternational.com).

WHERE TO VISIT

• VILLA DI CAPEZZANA AT CARMIGNANO, a 14th-century estate that now produces olive oil and wine, is open for tours by appointment. The villa also runs five-day culinary programs for 12 to 14 participants. Contact Villa di Capezzana (011-39-055-870-6005 or www.capezzana.it).

• VILLA DELIA, a 24-bedroom hotel and cooking school owned by Tuscan chef Umberto Menghi, is located in Ripoli de Lari, a small town about 25 minutes southeast of Pisa and about 45 minutes southwest of Florence. Contact Villa Delia (011-39-058-768-4322) or Umberto Management (604-669-3732 or www.umberto.com).

One of the reasons
to make pasta at home
is to include all the
fresh things growing
around you.

Penne tossed with tuna and capers.

After Luongo's cooking demonstration, everyone visits Napoléon's house on the island of Elba.

Warm Seafood Sandwiches

4 SERVINGS

- ¼ cup plus 2 tablespoons extra-virgin olive oil
- ¼ teaspoon crushed red pepper
- ½ pound cleaned small squid, cut into ½-inch rings
- 1 pound mussels, scrubbed and debearded
- 1½ pounds littleneck clams, scrubbed
- ½ cup water

One 24-inch baguette (10 ounces), ends trimmed

- 2 tablespoons fresh lemon juice
- 1 tablespoon chopped flat-leaf parsley

Salt and freshly ground pepper

1. In a large, deep skillet, heat 3 tablespoons of the olive oil until shimmering. Add the crushed red pepper and cook over high heat for 20 seconds to season the oil. Add the squid and cook, stirring, until opaque, about 1 minute. Using a slotted spoon, transfer the squid to a plate.

2. Add the mussels, clams and water to the skillet, cover and cook over high heat, stirring occasionally, until the shells open, 2 to 3 minutes for the mussels and 5 to 8 minutes for the clams. Transfer the mussels and clams to a large bowl as they open. Remove the mussels and clams from their shells and rinse briefly to remove any grit. On a work surface, coarsely chop the mussels, clams and squid.

3. Using a serrated knife, cut the baguette almost in half lengthwise, leaving one side attached. Scoop out the soft, white bread from the center of the baguette and tear it into ½-inch pieces.

4. Wipe out the skillet, add 1 tablespoon of olive oil and heat until shimmering. Add the bread pieces and cook over moderate heat, stirring constantly, until they are golden and crisp, about 5 minutes. Add the seafood, lemon juice, chopped parsley and the remaining 2 tablespoons of olive oil; season the seafood mixture with salt and pepper. Spoon the seafood mixture onto the baguette, cut the sandwich crosswise into 4 pieces and serve.

WINE A delicate, dry Italian Gavi with pronounced acidity will stand up to the brininess of the squid, mussels and clams in these sandwiches.

Garden Vegetable Panzanella

4 SERVINGS

Three ½-inch-thick slices of Tuscan bread, crusts removed and bread cut into ½-inch dice (5 cups)

- 2 tablespoons red wine vinegar

Salt

- ¼ cup extra-virgin olive oil

Freshly ground pepper

- 3 medium tomatoes, cut into 1-inch pieces
- 1 small cucumber—peeled, seeded and cut into ½-inch pieces
- ½ medium red or yellow bell pepper, cut into ½-inch strips
- 1 celery rib, cut into ½-inch pieces
- 3 scallions, white and tender green parts only, thinly sliced
- 4 ounces button mushrooms, trimmed and thinly sliced (2 cups)
- ¼ cup torn basil leaves

1. Preheat the oven to 300°. Spread the bread on a baking sheet and toast for 10 minutes. Let cool. Transfer to a large bowl.

2. In a small bowl, mix the vinegar with 1 teaspoon of salt until the salt dissolves. Slowly whisk in the olive oil and season the dressing with pepper.

Spaghetti alla Pirata includes mussels, clams and squid tossed in a lightly creamy tomato sauce.

3. Dip your fingers in water and flick them over the bread several times, tossing it with your hands until lightly moistened. Add the tomatoes, cucumber, bell pepper, celery, scallions, mushrooms and dressing and toss until evenly coated. Season the salad with salt and pepper, garnish with the basil and serve.

Penne with Tuna and Capers

4 SERVINGS

- ¾ **pound penne rigate**
- ¼ **cup extra-virgin olive oil**
- 3 **medium garlic cloves, smashed**
- One 6½-ounce can or jar of olive oil—packed tuna, drained and flaked
- ¼ **cup dry white wine**
- ¼ **cup drained capers**
- 2 **tablespoons very finely chopped flat-leaf parsley**

Salt and freshly ground pepper

1. Bring a large pot of salted water to a boil. Add the penne and cook until al dente. Drain the pasta, reserving ½ cup of the pasta cooking water.

2. Meanwhile, in a large skillet, heat the olive oil until shimmering. Add the garlic and cook over moderately high heat until golden, about

2 minutes. Add the drained tuna; cook for 1 minute. Add the white wine, capers and 1 tablespoon of the chopped parsley; season with salt and pepper. Cook the sauce until the wine has nearly evaporated, about 2 minutes longer. Add the penne and the reserved pasta water and cook, stirring, for 1 minute. Season with pepper, sprinkle with the remaining 1 tablespoon of parsley and serve.

Spaghetti alla Pirata

4 TO 6 SERVINGS

- 2 **tablespoons extra-virgin olive oil**
- 3 **garlic cloves, smashed**
- 1 **pound mussels, scrubbed and debearded**
- 1 **pound cockles or Manila clams, scrubbed**
- ¾ **cup dry white wine**
- 2 **cups canned tomato puree**
- 1 **tablespoon tomato paste**
- ¼ **teaspoon crushed red pepper**

Salt and freshly ground pepper

- 1 **pound small squid, cleaned and cut into ½-inch rings**
- ¼ **cup heavy cream**
- 1 **pound spaghetti**
- ¼ **cup torn basil leaves**

1. In a large flameproof casserole, heat the olive oil until shimmering. Add the smashed garlic cloves and cook over moderate heat, stirring, until golden, about 2 minutes. Add the mussels, cockles and wine. Cook over high heat, stirring, until some of the shells are open and the liquid has reduced by half, about 3 minutes. Add the tomato puree, tomato paste, crushed red pepper and a pinch each of salt and pepper; bring to a boil. Cook over high heat until the sauce thickens slightly, about 5 minutes. Stir in the squid, return the sauce to a boil and cook just until the squid is firm and opaque, about 30 seconds. Add the cream, reduce the heat to moderate and simmer for 1 minute. Season with salt and pepper.

2. Using a slotted spoon, transfer the seafood to a large serving platter. Boil the sauce over moderately high heat until reduced by half, about 10 minutes.

3. Meanwhile, cook the spaghetti in a large pot of boiling salted water until al dente; drain. Stir the spaghetti into the sauce and cook over moderate heat for 1 minute. Return the seafood to the pasta and toss well. Transfer the spaghetti to plates, garnish with the basil and serve.

WOLFGANG PUCK
Austria

TV chef Wolfgang Puck of Los Angeles's Spago got his first job at the Hotel Post in Villach, Austria. He'd already learned many classic Austrian dishes from his mother, Maria, who has passed away since her son's visit.

D id you know my mom taught me to cook?" Wolfgang Puck asked me at a luncheon a while back. "She was a professional chef—she cooked Austrian food at a resort hotel. She still lives in this little village where I grew up."

Really?

"Yes, in the same house."

I had known Puck was Austrian, of course, but this extra information struck me as irresistibly sweet. Of all celebrity chefs, Puck is the most glamorous and the most ubiquitous. The owner of Spago in Los Angeles turns up at the Academy Awards, on his Food Network show and in the freezer compartment at the A&P. He owns 12 white-tablecloth restaurants, with two new fine dining operations opening in Los Angeles and Atlantic City, plus the Hollywood ballroom and catering kitchen that is the new home of the Oscar ball. At last count, he had 11 Wolfgang Puck Cafés and 31 Wolfgang Puck Expresses, and he'd bet a Bentley that there will be 300 of the latter worldwide within five years' time.

That's why I'm thrilled to be standing in the Ernst Fuchs Palast Hotel ballroom in St. Veit, Carinthia (or Kärnten), Puck's hometown, listening to him address local journalists in his still

Puck left the quiet countryside behind to come to L.A. But the lessons of Austria's demanding, ingredient-obsessed chefs stayed with him.

"The food of our homeland can be very light and good."

WOLFGANG PUCK

distinctly Austrian accent. *"Grüss Gott,"* he begins, using the quaint Austrian greeting, and he embarks on a history of Puck, the American years, before being ceremonially presented with some local schnapps and a video of *Kärntner Lieder,* the songs of his youth.

Though he's visited before without too much hoopla, this time Puck has not slipped invisibly into his homeland. Yesterday, he says, the mayor of Vienna gave him this, and he opens a box to show me the *Goldener Rathaus Mann* ("gold town-hall man")—a golden homunculus—that is an honor, something like a key to the city. Tomorrow his name will be inscribed in the Golden Book of the city of Villach, where he had his first chef's post; a few hours later, at Wörther See, a choir of women in dirndls will yodel while two men in loden coats and lederhosen present him with a large carp. But that's tomorrow. Today we're in St. Veit, the town where Puck was born.

"It's funny," he says with a conspiratorial grin. (That smile, it turns out, is not merely for the cameras—it's natural.) "Now they all say they know me. This guy just said, 'Don't you remember me? We were in the military together!' Well"—now he's laughing—"I never was *in* the military..."

Other St. Veit citizens are probably just as hazy on the Puck biography, since his grandest successes have occurred on the other side of the Atlantic. And *grand* is the word. Trace the metamorphosis of public dining over the past 28 years and you quickly see how resounding the impact of Puck's work has been; the American restaurant scene would have developed very differently without him. California-French food, Asian fusion, designer pizzas, open kitchens, the chef as celebrity and Las Vegas as epicurean destination—all these phenomena were his fault. And none of them exist in the province of Carinthia. The most forward-looking restaurants in Austria are only now awakening to the Asian-fusion and pared-down-French food that this son of theirs brought to his adopted country some 20 years ago. Where did he get his ideas? From his mom? From cooking school in Villach? From Maxim's in Paris, where he did a stint in the '70s? I'm betting—no Bentley at stake—all of the above.

At the St. Veit press conference, Puck is singing the praises of Austrian dishes—the *Tafelspitz* and *Kaiserschmarren, Rindsgulasch* and *Sacher Torte* (boiled beef and sweet skillet soufflés, beef goulash and chocolate cake)—that he watched his mother make. "The food of our homeland can be very light and good," he tells them.

But do *you* cook Austrian food? I ask him afterward, disarmed by his fervor. "Oh, yes," he assures me: He's always served updated Austrian dishes at Spago. There's a version of his mother's *Kärntner Käsenudeln,* the local curd-cheese pasta, that he could never remove from the menu. He gets complaints if he tries.

Oh, my. And I thought I'd done my research.

Later, at the Puck family home, I discover another unforeseen link between Austria and America, then and now. The house is a perfect little Tyrolean chalet on a peaceful hillside

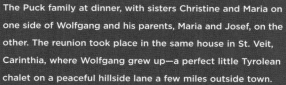

The Puck family at dinner, with sisters Christine and Maria on one side of Wolfgang and his parents, Maria and Josef, on the other. The reunion took place in the same house in St. Veit, Carinthia, where Wolfgang grew up—a perfect little Tyrolean chalet on a peaceful hillside lane a few miles outside town.

lane a few miles outside town. Upstairs, beneath sloping wooden eaves, lives Christine Puck, the elder of Puck's two younger sisters, a vivacious schoolteacher. Downstairs is a tiny, efficient kitchen with a Formica floor, a pine table and cupboards, and a cozy pine-paneled breakfast room adjoining. The living room—shades drawn against the sun at the moment, blocking the bucolic view—is furnished for the senior Pucks' comfort with a big squishy sofa and cabinets containing Prosecco glasses, a cut-crystal 80th-birthday stein, sports trophies, a small Eiffel Tower and Wolfgang smiling out from his latest book, *Pizza, Pasta and More!* The walls are crammed with photographs: the youngest Puck, Klaus, with his wife, Amanda Larsen-Puck; Wolfgang with President Clinton; with Madonna; with Michael Jackson; with the Reagans; with Barbara Lazaroff, his wife and business partner; with their sons, Cameron and Byron; on skis; on a German magazine cover beneath the headline *Der Koch als Millionär...* There's also a photograph of George Foreman, inscribed "To Josef. From one boxer to another."

So you can trace Wolfgang Puck's boxing fanaticism, and therefore the hot Las Vegas restaurant scene, to St. Veit: Josef—who adopted young Wolfgang when he was six, after his birth father had disappeared—is a former Austrian light- and welterweight champ. "Oh, sure," Puck confirms, as if this were common knowledge. "If I weren't so into boxing, I would never have opened in Vegas."

Josef Puck, at 86, is every bit the former athlete, compact and weathered and light on his feet. Near the thriving flower, herb and vegetable garden in back are dozens of cords of perfectly symmetrical firewood that he chopped himself, despite having lost one hand and several fingers of the other in a fireworks accident about 23 years ago. He sits close to his wife. It's hard to resist the impulse to hug Maria Puck, so tiny and beaming is she in her huge specs and *Willkommen Österreich* apron—and, in fact, I don't really have to resist, because within the hour she's considering me extended family. Presently, Maria joins their younger daughter, also named Maria—who teaches handicapped kids in the western province of Vorarlberg—to make dough for *Kärntner Käsenudeln,* the almost spherical curd-cheese-and-mint ravioli that are Frau Puck's specialty. Josef stays at the table, casting adoring glances at Wolfgang.

Josef Puck wasn't always so proud of his son. Our visit earlier in the day to the *Volksschule* Wolfgang attended from ages 5 to 10—a simple yellow schoolhouse surrounded by fields rolling down to Alpine foothills—had released a torrent of memories.

"I never had fun on my birthday," Puck told me. "It's in July, and that was around the time we had exams. Father would say, 'Go into the forest and pick a stick for me to beat you with.'" But he was smiling at the recollection. "You know, everyone was like that—that's the way punishment was at the time. Kids had to get up at 6 a.m. to feed the cows. We walked several miles to school. It was harder then."

While Wolfgang starts his share of the cooking, I chat with Christine and a family friend and fellow chef, Mike Koeberl. "He's so cool," Mike says. "I never saw Wolfgang mad."

A lake near the Puck family home
is popular for fishing and splashing.

"Never ever ever," Christine shakes her head. "He tells me he gets mad, but I've never seen it."

When Wolfgang decided at the age of 14 to become a chef, they tell me, his father was extremely displeased.

"Our father worked the mines," Christine says. "He had to feed the family. He said a man should work—men should not be in the kitchen."

I turn to Herr Puck, who speaks no English. "What did you want your son to be?" I ask. Josef Puck is clearly delighted when Christine translates.

"He says he wanted him to build houses," Christine interprets. "But then, with *Nudeln* he did build a house." Herr Puck is chortling away. "He says a chef can't build a house with bricks, but it's better this way. He says men *have* to be in the kitchen!" It was when Spago opened, in 1982, they tell me, that Josef Puck came up with this line.

In the kitchen, Frau Puck is mixing curd cheese, egg yolk, potato and minced herbs for the *Nudeln* while her son chops up a small Alp of produce from out back—leeks, kohlrabi, carrots, zucchini, potatoes, onions—for the freshest-ever vegetable soup.

When I ask about his first dish, Maria recalls the marble cake that 10-year-old Wolfgang baked her for Mother's Day—"It was very good." And yes, she says, she always thought he'd be a chef, because it comes from deep in his heart. When Wolfgang was a child, Maria Puck was a chef at the Hotel Linde in Wörther See, some 20 miles away, and her eldest would visit her in the summer.

You must have learned a lot there, I say.

"Well, when you're young, you like sweets," Puck replies. "I became friendly with the pastry chef." His interest must have been noted, though, because Maria's boss, the hotel owner, got Wolfgang his first job, at a hotel nearby. "My mother pulled strings," Puck says. "It was hard to get jobs in the early '60s."

The next day we visit the scene of that first job: the Hotel Post, Villach, a romantic 15th-century palace. But it doesn't hold much romance for Puck. "It's a funny feeling," he tells me, sotto voce. We're surrounded by local dignitaries, here for the Mayor's Golden Book commemoration of the visit. "In Villach I wasn't happy. It wasn't easy." Puck is visibly shaken. He's just run into his former boss, a man who made his life miserable and sacked him after six weeks. "He never liked me, because the manager of the Linde said he had to take me," Puck remembers. He was just 14 and looked young for his age. "Chef said, 'You should go back to your mother—she should breast-feed you so you grow a bit.'" The prospect of his father's wrath tortured him. "I said, 'There's a bridge over there—I'm going to kill myself.' But the other chefs told me if I hid out in the cellar I could peel the potatoes for them. So I lived in the cellar, and they smuggled me food." When he was discovered, his dedication to the work won him a new job at the neighboring Park Hotel, and things started to look up. Cooking school followed. His class won the province of Carinthia's highest culinary prize in 1967, and Puck won the individual gold medal. One of his teachers, Franz Berger—who has joined us today—took a particular interest

Wolfgang Puck uses ultrafresh paprika for his beef goulash with spaetzle.

in his star pupil, encouraging him to accept an internship in France. There the still-teenage Puck consolidated his mastery of the classical French canon—the next building block he would bring to America. He was dreaming of America even in Villach, he says.

He's only been back here a couple of times, and never to the Hotel Post kitchens. The cellar, it turns out, is still dank and dark. When Puck ducks inside, mugging for comic effect, I think I see disquiet, too; it's a poignant, private moment, the small and frightened boy he was last time he was here superimposed on his familiar famous face.

Before Herr and Frau Puck and Christine join us for a festive dinner at an old friend's restaurant, the Gasthof Tschebull, in nearby Faaker See, we drive to the lake for a spot of fishing, laid on especially for Puck. Then it's the yodeling choir and carp presentation, filmed by Austrian ORF TV news.

"I don't like to be on TV," Puck admits—somewhat surprisingly for a man with his own show on the Food Network—"but I'm getting used to it." Finally, the family sits down to a grand repast of *Sauersuppe,* a rich meat soup, and *Reindling,* a yeast cake with cinnamon and raisins. We have pork with mounds of local chanterelles and a kind of misshapen gnocchi, then steamed apple dumplings with vanilla-*Apfelwein* sauce—all washed down with a Friuli Latisana, its labels specially painted and printed for today by Berger, the cooking-school teacher. Wolfgang eats the lot, with a gusto that reminds me to ask him how he's managed to get so trim lately. He says he's been taking his kids to school every morning—part of his resolve to spend more time with them—and walking the four miles back.

Hmm, I say. Running the restaurants, two huge new projects, an expanding café empire, a TV show, traveling... Where do you get all this stamina?

"Restaurants," he declares, "are energy training."

I glance across the table, at Maria and Josef Puck, who are glowing with joy. Aren't you tired today after all that cooking? I ask Maria. She shrugs: *"Ach! Das macht nichts"*—it was nothing. It's midnight. My forehead is on the table. Maria Puck, nearly 80, accepts another glass of wine, as ebullient as a teenager. Wolfgang Puck may have drawn his menus from his homeland, but the spark that ignites them? It's in the genes.

BY KATE SEKULES

TRAVEL TIPS

- Author Kate Sekules flew to Vienna on SWISS INTERNATIONAL AIRLINES (877-FLY-SWISS), then to Klagenfurt on Tyrolean Airways, a division of Austrian Airlines (800-843-0002).

- The ERNST FUCHS PALAST, a spectacular Gaudiesque "Art Hotel," is a landmark in St. Veit. Both it and the very romantic HOTEL POST in Villach make fine bases for exploring Carinthia.

- No one should miss the 14th-century hilltop CASTLE BURG HOCHOSTERWITZ, eight miles from St. Veit. (For details, contact the Austrian National Tourist Office; 212-944-6880.)

Beef Goulash with Spaetzle

6 SERVINGS

The paprika for this nicely spicy beef goulash (a dish Austria assimilated from Hungary), should be as fresh as possible.

- 1 tablespoon caraway seeds
- 2 tablespoons extra-virgin olive oil
- 2 large onions, thinly sliced
- 1 tablespoon sugar
- 3 garlic cloves, minced
- 3 tablespoons sweet Hungarian paprika
- 1 teaspoon hot Hungarian paprika
- 2 tablespoons minced marjoram
- 1 teaspoon minced thyme
- 1 bay leaf
- 3 tablespoons tomato paste
- 4 cups chicken stock or canned low-sodium broth
- 2 ½ pounds trimmed boneless chuck, cut into 2-inch pieces

Salt and freshly ground pepper

Spaetzle (recipe follows)

1. In a small skillet, toast the caraway seeds over moderate heat until darkened and fragrant, about 1 minute. Transfer to a spice grinder and let cool, then grind to a powder.
2. Heat the olive oil in a large, enameled cast-iron casserole. Add the onions and sugar and cook over moderate heat, stirring occasionally, until the onions are evenly browned, about 20 minutes. Add the garlic and ground caraway and cook, stirring, for 1 minute. Add the sweet paprika, hot paprika, marjoram, thyme and bay leaf and cook, stirring, until fragrant, about 2 minutes. Stir in the tomato paste and then the chicken stock. Add the chuck, season with

salt and pepper and simmer until the meat is very tender, about 2 hours. Skim off the fat, season the goulash with salt and pepper and serve with the Spaetzle.

MAKE AHEAD The goulash can be refrigerated for up to 2 days.

Spaetzle

6 SERVINGS

- 4 large egg yolks
- 1 large egg
- 1 ¾ cups milk
- 3 ½ cups all-purpose flour

Salt and freshly ground pepper

- ¼ teaspoon freshly grated nutmeg
- ¼ cup peanut oil
- 2 tablespoons unsalted butter
- 1 tablespoon minced parsley

1. In a small bowl, whisk the egg yolks with the whole egg and milk. In a large bowl, mix the flour with 1 teaspoon of salt, ¼ teaspoon of pepper and the nutmeg. Add the egg mixture and stir just until blended; do not overmix. Cover the batter and refrigerate for at least 1 hour and up to 4 hours.
2. Bring a large pot of salted water to a boil. Using a rubber spatula and working over the pot, push the batter into the boiling water through a colander with large holes, stopping once or twice to stir the water. Cook until the spaetzle are tender, about 4 minutes; drain.
3. In a large skillet, heat the oil until shimmering. Add the spaetzle and cook over moderately high heat, without stirring, until beginning to brown on the bottom, about 3 minutes. Add the butter and cook, stirring occasionally, until golden brown, about 2 minutes longer. Season with salt and pepper, sprinkle with the parsley and serve.

Chicken in Paprika Cream Sauce

6 SERVINGS

In Austria, this old-fashioned dish is traditionally served to celebrate anniversaries. You can make it with all white meat if you prefer (use six breast halves).

- 2 teaspoons caraway seeds
- 1 red bell pepper

Three ½-pound skinless, boneless chicken breast halves, each cut crosswise into 3 pieces

- 3 whole chicken legs, cut into drumsticks and thighs

Salt and freshly ground pepper

- 2 tablespoons sweet Hungarian paprika

All-purpose flour, for dusting

- 3 tablespoons peanut oil
- 2 medium onions, thinly sliced
- 3 large garlic cloves, minced
- 1 medium tomato—peeled, seeded and chopped
- 2 tablespoons minced marjoram
- 1 tablespoon tomato paste
- 1 teaspoon minced thyme
- 1 bay leaf
- ½ cup dry white wine
- 1 ½ cups chicken stock or canned low-sodium broth
- ¼ cup plus 2 tablespoons crème fraîche
- 2 tablespoons minced parsley

1. In a small skillet, toast the caraway seeds over moderate heat until fragrant, about 1 minute. Transfer the seeds to a spice grinder, let cool completely, then grind to a powder.
2. Roast the red pepper directly over an open flame or in the broiler, turning, until charred all over. Put the pepper in a bowl,

On his homecoming trip, Wolfgang Puck raided the garden with his mother for a traditional feast.

cover with plastic and let steam for 10 minutes. Discard the skin, stem and seeds and cut the pepper into ¼-inch strips.

3. Season the chicken with salt and pepper and dust with 1 tablespoon of the paprika. Lightly dust the chicken with flour. Heat the oil in a large enameled cast-iron casserole. Add the chicken in batches and cook over moderately high heat until browned, about 2 minutes per side. Transfer to a large plate.

4. Add the onions and garlic to the casserole and cook over moderate heat, stirring, until softened, 5 minutes. Add the ground caraway and the remaining 1 tablespoon of paprika and cook, stirring, until fragrant, 2 minutes. Add the tomato, marjoram, tomato paste, thyme and bay leaf and cook, stirring, for 1 minute. Stir in the wine and simmer for 1 minute. Add the stock, season with salt and pepper and bring to a simmer.

5. Return the chicken to the casserole along with any accumulated juices. Cover and simmer over low heat until the breast pieces are cooked through; start checking after 10 minutes. Transfer to a plate. Continue simmering until the drumsticks and thighs are cooked through and tender, about 15 more minutes; transfer to the plate.

6. Add ¼ cup of the crème fraîche to the sauce and simmer for 5 minutes. Discard the bay leaf. Working in batches, puree the hot sauce in a blender with half of the roasted pepper strips. Return the chicken to the casserole and pour the sauce on top. Bring to a simmer and season with salt and pepper. Transfer the chicken to a serving bowl. Drizzle the remaining 2 tablespoons of crème fraîche over the chicken, then garnish with the remaining pepper strips, sprinkle with the parsley and serve.

SERVE WITH Rice or spaetzle.

MAKE AHEAD The chicken stew can be refrigerated overnight. Reheat gently.

WINE The sweet, smoky paprika and smooth, creamy sauce will flatter the ripe fruit and soft texture of an Austrian Riesling.

Wolfgang's Sacher Torte

MAKES ONE 9-INCH CAKE

CAKE

- 6 **ounces bittersweet chocolate, finely chopped**
- 6 **tablespoons unsalted butter**
- 4 **large eggs, separated**
- ½ **cup sugar**
- ⅓ **cup all-purpose flour**
- 1 **large egg white**
- ¼ **teaspoon salt**
- ½ **cup apricot preserves**
- 1½ **teaspoons apricot brandy**

GLAZE

- 6 **ounces bittersweet chocolate, finely chopped**
- 2 **tablespoons unsalted butter**
- ¼ **cup heavy cream**

1. MAKE THE CAKE: Preheat the oven to 350°. Butter and flour a 9-inch round cake pan. In the top of a double boiler, melt the chocolate with the butter; let cool.

2. In a medium bowl, using an electric mixer, beat the 4 egg yolks with 3 tablespoons of the sugar until light, 5 minutes. Beat in the melted chocolate; gently fold in the flour.

3. In another large bowl, using clean beaters, beat the 5 egg whites with the salt until soft peaks form. Add the remaining 5 tablespoons of sugar and beat until firm and glossy. Fold one-third of the beaten whites into the chocolate mixture to lighten it, then fold in the remaining whites until incorporated. Scrape the batter into the prepared pan and bake for 40 minutes, or until a cake tester inserted in the center comes out clean. Transfer to a rack to cool.

Kaiserschmarren, or skillet soufflés, are an airy Viennese dessert. Puck pairs his with a sweet plum compote.

4. Puree the apricot preserves in a food processor, then blend in the brandy.

5. MAKE THE GLAZE: In a small stainless steel bowl set over a small saucepan of simmering water, melt the chocolate with the butter. In another small saucepan, bring the cream to a boil. Stir it into the melted chocolate and let the shiny glaze cool until warm.

6. Run a thin knife around the edge of the cake to loosen it. Turn the cake out onto a cake rack set over a baking sheet; let cool. Using a serrated knife, cut the cake in half horizontally. Spread the apricot preserves evenly over a cut side and set the second layer on top. Slowly and evenly pour the chocolate glaze over the cake, using a metal offset spatula to spread it evenly over the top and around the sides; any excess glaze will drip into the pan below. With a large, wide spatula, transfer the cake to a platter and refrigerate to firm the glaze, about 30 minutes. Cut the cake with a warmed knife.

SERVE WITH Whipped cream.

MAKE AHEAD The glazed cake can be refrigerated for up to 5 days.

COFFEE Instead of wine, serve this Austrian chocolate cake with a strong Viennese coffee topped with plenty of whipped cream.

Skillet Soufflés
with Plum Compote

6 SERVINGS

The batter for *Kaiserschmarren,* this Viennese dessert, is delicate, but that doesn't mean these soufflés are challenging to make: They taste good whether they're soft in the middle or cooked to a crisp. The sugar sprinkled in the skillets helps the soufflés rise.

- 3 **tablespoons golden raisins**
- ½ **cup granulated sugar**
- 2 **large eggs, separated**
- ½ **cup crème fraîche**
- 2 **tablespoons dark rum**
- 3 **tablespoons all-purpose flour, sifted**
- 4 **large egg whites**

Confectioners' sugar, for dusting
Plum Compote (recipe follows)

1. Preheat the oven to 425°. In a small saucepan, cover the raisins with water and bring to a boil; set aside until softened, about 10 minutes. Drain the raisins and pat dry.

2. Butter two 8-inch ovenproof skillets and sprinkle each with 1 tablespoon of the granulated sugar; shake to coat the bottoms and sides. In a medium bowl, using an electric mixer, beat the 2 egg yolks with ¼ cup of the granulated sugar until thick and pale, about 5 minutes. Beat in the crème fraîche and then the rum. Fold in the flour and raisins.

3. In a stainless steel bowl, beat the 6 egg whites until soft peaks form. Add the remaining 2 tablespoons of granulated sugar and beat until firm and glossy. Fold the whites into the egg yolk mixture. Pour the batter into the skillets and bake for 12 minutes, or until the soufflés have risen and are golden. Spoon onto 6 plates, dust with confectioners' sugar and serve with the Plum Compote.

WINE A lusciously rich late-harvest wine with good acidity will complement this light soufflé and add a refreshing citrusy note.

Plum Compote

6 SERVINGS

- 1 **cup sugar**
- ½ **cup water**
- 9 **red plums, halved and pitted**
- 1 **tablespoon fresh lemon juice**

In a saucepan, bring the sugar and water to a boil. Add the plums, cover and simmer over low heat, turning once, until the plums are tender but still hold their shape, about 10 minutes. Stir in the lemon juice and let cool. Serve warm or at room temperature.

BARAK HIRSCHOWITZ
& DYLAN PRITCHARD
South Africa

Wine expert Dylan Pritchard, seated, and chef Barak Hirschowitz lead a South African food safari that takes in cities, wine country, bushveld and beach. OPPOSITE: Royal Malewane lodge in Kruger National Park.

t was a big Cabernet Sauvignon. Big enough to fill a bathtub. I'd come to South Africa to soak up the country's thriving wine and food scene and found myself soaking *in* it. Up to my nose in a cask-shaped hot tub in the vinotherapy room of the Santé Winelands Hotel and Wellness Center near Cape Town, I wondered at all the changes this country had seen. Six years ago, in the wake of apartheid, you wouldn't have found much in the way of culinary tourism here, even though the green hills and valleys of nearby Franschhoek and Stellenbosch are among the world's most beautiful wine-producing lands. The success of a revolution is probably best judged by more important factors than the quality of the meals (and spa treatments) on offer. But I'll take it as a good sign that the country is becoming a luxury-travel destination, that Franschhoek—where dissident French Huguenots planted some of South Africa's first vines, in the late 1600s—is attracting talented winemakers and chefs and that Cape Town's and Johannesburg's restaurants are packed.

It would be hard to find two people who better symbolize South Africa's culinary future than Barak Hirschowitz and Dylan Pritchard. Barak, who owns a chef recruitment and place-ment company, is one of the country's great chefs. He got his start at the Tides restaurant,

On Gourmet African Tours, travelers visit big-game safari camps in Kruger National Park and trendy lounges like Planet Champagne Bar in Cape Town, OPPOSITE.

ingeniously using local ingredients to create delicious modern South African dishes, such as kingklip, a halibut-like fish, topped with a tangy sauce made of green olives from the Cape. Dylan is the food and beverage director at the Mount Nelson Hotel in Cape Town. The two are ludicrously well informed and patriotically enthusiastic about all things South African. Since it's impossible to get the word out about the massive transformation happening in South Africa by staying in the kitchen, the two have started a travel company, Gourmet African Tours, leading small groups on customized trips around the country. The aim is not just to eat and drink (although guests will be doing plenty of both) but also to meet and hang out with South Africa's most important chefs and winemakers.

Just before the Gourmet African Tours launch, Barak and Dylan took me on a test run. Our plan was simple: Drive and eat, travel from restaurant to winery to game reserve and never let more than a few minutes go by between meals. In other words: a food lover's perfect African safari.

Outside the Santé Winelands Hotel and Wellness Centre, the sun shone down on grapes nearly ready for picking; inside, my skin had just been rubbed with a vigorous Shiraz Body Scrub, a fragrant mixture of crushed grapes and coarse salt. I couldn't help thinking that, with the addition of a little rosemary, I'd make a delicious roast. Pleasant as it was to be marinating in my barrel bath after the body scrub, I was eager to shower and be on my way.

We'd kicked off our tour the night before with a toast at Planet Champagne Bar, a clubby lounge inside Cape Town's Mount Nelson Hotel, where locals and visitors sat sipping bubbly cocktails at a glowing, underlit onyx bar. "A few years ago, the city couldn't have sustained a place like this," Barak had told me as we drank cocktails made with Champagne, brandy and Angostura bitters. After drinks at Planet, Barak and Dylan had ushered me off to dinner at the Africa Café, a raucous celebration of pan-African food and culture. Drummers roamed through the exuberantly painted multistory house. We didn't order so much as submit to the torrent of dishes representing the traditional cuisines of Ethiopia, Kenya and, of course, South Africa. I filled up on juicy Cape mussels with Malay curry, spicy Ethiopian *zambossa* (minced meat in pastry) and Botswanan ostrich.

The next morning, Barak and Dylan picked me up early for our drive to the cluster of towns known collectively as the Winelands. Barak sat in the back seat, talking fast and delivering running commentary on both the swiftly passing countryside and the state of South African cookery. Dylan was behind the wheel, driving fast and interrupting Barak to brief me on South African wines. My metabolism and I tried to keep up.

The drive from Cape Town takes less than an hour. Leaving behind Table Mountain and the coast, you pass into a region of orchards and farms with old white houses in the gabled Cape Dutch style. After our stop at the Santé Winelands Hotel & Wellness Centre, we headed to Clos Malverne, one of South Africa's top wineries; here, Dylan wanted me to taste specimens of what has become known as a Cape Blend, which includes a certain percentage of the

Outside Cape Town are orchards and farms with old white houses in gabled Cape Dutch style and Mediterranean crops.

Our plan was simple: Drive and eat, travel from restaurant to winery to game reserve and never let more than a few minutes go by between meals.

Table Mountain looms above Cape Town.

Luxurious Royal Malewane lodge. OPPOSITE: **Hirschowitz's roasted halibut with a tangy green-olive sauce.**

indigenous Pinotage grape, a cross between Pinot Noir and Cinsaut. Calling a wine like Clos Malverne Auret a Cape Blend is meant to emphasize its South Africanness. There has been some controversy about whether it's necessary for every wine labeled a Cape Blend to include Pinotage, a debate that's easy to ignore when one is preoccupied with a glass of the stuff, especially Clos Malverne's 2001 Limited Release and the award-sweeping, utterly satisfying 2001 Cabernet Sauvignon Merlot Limited Release.

t's easy to get slowed down tasting wine, and we were a little late for lunch at Le Quartier Français, a Relais & Châteaux inn known for its mountain views and its amiable, talented young Dutch-born chef, Margot Janse. The price we paid for being late was not being able to linger as long as we would have liked over the six-course meal. The first taste of cured quail with wispy bits of zucchini and Parmesan confirmed that we should have come earlier and stayed through dinner, and maybe breakfast. Barak and Margot talked about the importance of South African ingredients. "South Africa has always been a huge exporter—seafood to Europe, porcini mushrooms to the U.S., tuna for canning to Mexico and Australia—but for years everything was shipped out of the country, too expensive to use here," Barak said. Now that the rand has stabilized somewhat and tourism has increased, restaurants are finding an appreciative audience.

After the quail dish, Margot brought out a loin of springbok—a hopping antelope and the national emblem—wrapped in bacon and served with fried asparagus. Springbok has the kind of texture I imagine you'd get if you mated a tuna with a lamb. It makes you wonder why we Americans put up with so much boring purple venison. Margot paired the springbok with a 2001 Kevin Arnold Shiraz, which had the kind of fine, smooth-spicy balance that makes you want to shake the winemaker's hand.

As it turned out, Barak and Dylan had arranged for Kevin Arnold to meet us for lunch. Arnold's winery, Waterford, opened seven years ago and has been making a name for itself with its Shiraz, Cabernet Sauvignon and a none-too-oaky Chardonnay. (Oprah Winfrey served his Shiraz at her 50th-birthday party last year.) Now, Arnold said, is the

time for South Africa to produce a truly great wine: "I want to make something that will be for us like Grange is for Australia."

After a dessert of cappuccino cheesecake, we got back in the car, and Dylan explained to me why South Africa is poised to start making world-class wines. "Our soils and our coastal influences have all aided the reds—like Pinotage and Shiraz—which have come into their own over the last few years," he said. "Chardonnay and Sauvignon Blanc from Europe and New Zealand develop unique personalities here. They're more masculine. The fruit comes through powerfully, and wine farmers here have learned not to kill the fruit with overoaking." Dylan explained that Afrikaners used to like their wine sticky sweet, so decades ago, farmers replaced most of their vines with ones that produce Chenin Blanc and Sémillon grapes, which are used to make sweet wines. This created a stagnant, one-dimensional wine industry. Everywhere around us was evidence of its resurgence.

In the early evening, we pulled in to La Residence, an exquisitely turned out five-room inn in Franschhoek. Built around a courtyard pool, the house is Mediterranean in inspiration, but its mixed-heritage design is distinctly South African. The rooms have marble baths, French furniture and perfect views of Franschhoek Valley. Drinking Cape Classique (South Africa's answer to *méthode champenoise*) from nearby Cabrière Estate, we stared at the gorgeous, backlit mountain peaks.

The three holiest words in South Africa's culinary tradition are *biltong, sundowner* and *braai.* Respectively, these refer to air-dried meat, a sunset cocktail and an outdoor barbecue, the preferred form of social communion. *Biltong* and beef jerky are both salt-cured meat snacks, just as Champagne and Schlitz are both refreshing carbonated beverages. But you wouldn't want to say that to a Frenchman or a South African.

To experience a true Afrikaner *braai,* we drove west to the Atlantic coast to Yzerfontein, a dusty, dinky *dorp* (Afrikaans for country village). At Strandkombuis restaurant, we found *braai* central—a complex of barbecue pit, stone ovens and picnic tables set at one end of a magnificent 16-mile beach. Afrikaners traditionally begin every festive meal with bread and jam. With this bread (cooked in one of the wood-burning ovens) and these syrupy jams (fig, apricot, grape), I would too. Next, we had a delicious roasted Cape lobster and *snoek,* a hot-smoked fish eaten on the doughy bread and jam. Dylan asked for some *bokkoms*—salted mullets, dried in the sun. From the amused looks at the tables around us, I got the feeling *bokkoms* might not be a delicacy dear to younger generations of Afrikaners.

In the interest of rounding out my education, Barak and Dylan had signed me up for a class at the Institute of Culinary Arts just outside Stellenbosch. Here I was issued an apron, a glass of home-fermented ginger beer and instruction in the art of the *bobotie*. A cross between meat loaf and shepherd's pie but with a custardy topping, *bobotie* is one of South Africa's national dishes, displaying a blend of Dutch and Cape Malay influences. Since this was adult education and not vocational training, I sat back with the

MENU
Bread - hot from the oven
West Coast fish soup

Calamari   Mussels
Greek Salad, Cole Slaw
and Tomato, Egg, Onion Salad

Yellow tail fillets,
Smoked snoek, Crayfish

Coffee and Koeksisters

Beyond occasionally spotting big game such as a sleeping lion stretched out on the ground, one of the joys of a South African food safari is exploring local ingredients both inland and on the Atlantic coast.

The tour stops at safari camps, resorts and restaurants. OPPOSITE: A waitress at Cape Town's Africa Café.

beer as a student chef pulled a finished, fragrant *bobotie* from the oven.

Once I'd soaked in wine and experienced a seaside *braai,* learned to bake a *bobotie* and eaten smoked *snoek,* there was nothing left but to leave the Cape in search of the perfect sun-downer. Any South African will agree that the ideal evening cocktail is one enjoyed deep in the bush after a long day tracking big game. We flew to Johannesburg, then stopped for a lunch of African breads and more *bobotie* at Moyo, a cavernous, popular African-themed restaurant.

From Jo'burg we drove five hours to the tip of Kruger National Park, eating *biltong* all the way. Two hours outside the first game reserve, we came across a baboon standing in

TRAVEL TIPS

HOW TO GET THERE
• SOUTH AFRICAN AIRWAYS flies directly to Johannesburg daily from New York City and to Johannesburg and Cape Town from Atlanta (866-722-2476 or flysaa.com). GOURMET AFRICAN TOURS offers customized culinary tours throughout South Africa (from $5,000 for a 12-day tour; WAYFARER TRAVEL SERVICES; 800-638-5351 or www.gourmetafrica.net).

WHERE TO STAY
• CAPE HERITAGE HOTEL A lovely hotel in a restored downtown building
(doubles from $200; 90 Bree St., Cape Town; 011-27-21-424-4646).
• THE WESTCLIFF A castlelike compound on a hill
(doubles from $340; 67 Jan Smuts Ave., Westcliff; 011-27-11-646-2400).
• LA RESIDENCE Small exquisite inn near wineries
(doubles from $500; Domaine Des Anges, Dirkie Uys St., Franschhoek; 011-27-15-793-0150).
• SANTÉ WINELANDS HOTEL & WELLNESS CENTER Wine-region resort with vinotherapy spa treatments
(doubles from $450; Farm Simonsvlei, Klapmuts, Simondium; 011-27-21-875-8100).
• NGALA TENTED SAFARI CAMP Upscale camp in Kruger National Park
(from $600 per person; Ngala Private Game Reserve; 011-27-11-809-4300).
• ROYAL MALEWANE LODGE Elegant safari camp; each guest suite has a private pool
(from $1,000 per person; Thorny Bush Game Reserve, Hoedspruit; 011-27-15-793-0150).

Franschhoek's vineyards and mountain views.

A Cape-style farmhouse; Africa Café's Sesame-Coated Sweet Potato Croquettes; inside Royal Malewane.

a tree. It occurred to me then that I hadn't fully prepared my city-boy self for what was to come: cheetahs and rhinos, delicate zebras and massive, imbecilic Cape buffalo. Our first camp was Royal Malewane, a beautiful, ritzy place where the elephants sometimes drink out of the suites' private pools. We fell into the rhythm of the typical safari camp—a 5 a.m. rise for a drive, then breakfast, a nap while the big cats slept in the afternoon and then another three-hour drive at night. On one drive we came across a pride of lions devouring what was left of a buck they'd taken down a few hours before. Our day ended in a carnivorous spirit too, with a dinner of barbecued ostrich and kudu (a kind of antelope).

Our finest sundowner came the next day, at the luxurious Ngala Tented Camp, after an afternoon of hide-and-seek with a drowsy leopard. Leopards are notoriously hard to track, and it's rare to see one up close. As the light was fading, our guide heard the warning shouts of monkeys and followed their sound. We found the leopard sitting under a tree; he watched us calmly, yawning to show off his incredible teeth, and then walked to within a foot of our car before sauntering off into grasses too thick and dark for us to follow him. No gin and tonic has ever tasted better than the one that night.

BY ADAM SACHS

TRAVEL TIPS

WHERE TO EAT

• THE AFRICA CAFÉ Pan-African food, music and dancing (108 Shortmarket St., Cape Town; 011-27-21-422-0221).

• THE INSTITUTE OF CULINARY ARTS Classes in classic and modern South African cuisine (Annandale Rd., Lynedoch, Stellenbosch; 011-27-21-881-3443).

• LE QUARTIER FRANÇAIS Modern French cuisine made with local ingredients (16 Huguenot Rd., Franschhoek; 011-27-21-876-2151).

• MOYO Popular restaurant serving classic South African food (5 Melrose Sq., Johannesburg; 011-27-11-684-1477).

• PLANET CHAMPAGNE BAR Trendy lounge in the Mount Nelson Hotel (76 Orange St., Cape Town; 011-27-21-483-1864).

Sesame-Coated Sweet Potato Croquettes

MAKES ABOUT 30 CROQUETTES

At the Africa Café in Cape Town, diners sit down to communal feasts by chef and co-owner Portia de Smidt. The Pan-African offerings might include these delicious fried yam balls from Malawi, a small country north of South Africa. De Smidt refines the recipe and accentuates its origins by rolling the balls in sesame seeds, a typically Malawian ingredient.

1½   pounds sweet potatoes, peeled and cut into 2-inch chunks

Salt

¼   cup plus 2 tablespoons cornstarch

1   tablespoon sugar

½   teaspoon cinnamon

½   teaspoon ground allspice

6   ounces extra-sharp cheddar cheese, shredded (2 cups)

One 2-ounce jar sesame seeds (¾ cup)

Vegetable oil, for frying

1. Put the sweet potatoes in a medium saucepan, cover with water and bring to a boil. Add a large pinch of salt and simmer over moderately high heat until tender, about 20 minutes. Drain the sweet potatoes and return them to the pan. Shake the pan over high heat to dry out the potatoes, about 1 minute.

2. Mash the potatoes until smooth. Stir in the cornstarch, sugar, cinnamon, allspice and cheddar. Season with salt.

3. Put the sesame seeds in a shallow bowl. Using your hands, roll the sweet potato mixture into 1-inch balls. Roll the balls in the sesame seeds until coated.

4. In each of 2 large skillets, heat ¼ inch of oil. Add the sweet potato balls and fry over moderate heat until golden brown all over, about 1 minute per side. Drain on paper towels. Serve the croquettes warm or at room temperature.

MAKE AHEAD The coated sweet potato balls can be refrigerated overnight. Remove them from the refrigerator at least 30 minutes before frying.

Asparagus and Smoked-Salmon Tart

8 SERVINGS

The Franschhoek Valley is full of farms raising salmon trout, a kind of trout with salmon-colored flesh that is one of the region's specialties. Barak Hirschowitz of Tides restaurant at the Bay Hotel in Cape Town uses the smoked fillets to add an earthy, salty flavor to his spring tart, but readily available smoked salmon makes a fine substitute.

PASTRY

1¼   cups all-purpose flour

Pinch of kosher salt

1   stick (4 ounces) unsalted butter, cut into small pieces and chilled

5   tablespoons ice water

FILLING

¾   pound pencil-thin asparagus

1   cup heavy cream

2   large egg yolks

1   large egg

½   teaspoon salt

¼   teaspoon freshly ground pepper

¼   pound thinly sliced smoked salmon or smoked salmon trout, cut into ½-inch strips

1. MAKE THE PASTRY: In a large bowl, mix the flour and salt. Using a pastry blender or 2 knives, cut in the butter until the mixture resembles coarse meal. Sprinkle on the ice water and toss with a fork to evenly moisten. Pat it into a disk. Cover with plastic wrap and refrigerate until firm, about 1 hour.

2. Preheat the oven to 350°. On a lightly floured surface, roll the pastry out to a 13-inch round about ⅛ inch thick. Fold the round in half and transfer it to an 11-inch fluted tart pan with a removable bottom. Unfold the pastry and gently press it into the pan without stretching. Trim off any overhanging pastry and refrigerate the shell for 30 minutes.

3. Line the shell with foil and fill with pie weights. Bake for 40 minutes, or until the edge starts to brown. Remove the foil and weights and bake for 10 minutes, or until golden. Reduce the temperature to 325°.

4. MAKE THE FILLING: In a medium saucepan of boiling salted water, cook the asparagus until tender, about 3 minutes. Drain and pat dry. Cut the asparagus into 1-inch lengths.

5. In a medium bowl, whisk the cream with the egg yolks and whole egg and season with the salt and pepper. Scatter the asparagus and the smoked salmon strips in the pastry shell. Carefully pour the custard into the shell and bake for about 30 minutes, or until the custard is set. Transfer the tart to a rack and let cool slightly before unmolding and serving.

MAKE AHEAD The tart can be prepared up to 8 hours ahead.

WINE A full-flavored Stellenbosch Chardonnay will complement the creamy filling and rich salmon here.

Face-painting at Africa Café; pot bread, served at a barbecue; an outdoor breakfast at a safari camp.

Grilled Whole Fish with Curried Yogurt Marinade

4 SERVINGS

Western coast cooks are masters of the fish *braai* (barbecue). At the Strandkombuis restaurant in Yzerfontein, the meal is a bit like a clambake in that chef and owner Marie van der Merwe grills all kinds of seafood over wood coals on the beach. This recipe, with its marinade and sweet spices, reflects the Cape Malay cooking style.

1½ cups plain whole-milk yogurt
 ½ cup chopped cilantro
  2 tablespoons fresh lime juice
  1 tablespoon curry powder
 ½ teaspoon ground ginger
  1 tablespoon extra-virgin olive oil
Four 1¼-pound sea bass or pompano, pan-dressed
Salt and freshly ground pepper

1. In a medium bowl, mix the yogurt with the cilantro, lime juice, curry powder, ginger and olive oil.

2. Make 3 crosswise slashes on both sides of each fish, cutting down to the bone. Transfer the fish to a large rimmed baking sheet and coat all over with the yogurt marinade. Cover and refrigerate for 1 to 2 hours.

3. Light a grill. Oil the grate. Remove the fish from the marinade, leaving on a light coating; reserve the marinade. Season the fish with salt and pepper and grill it over a medium-hot fire, basting occasionally with the marinade, until lightly charred and just cooked through, about 10 minutes per side. Serve right away.

WINE An assertive Stellenbosch Sauvignon Blanc with acidity will stand up to the fish's smoky grilled flavors.

Roasted Halibut with Green Olive Sauce

6 SERVINGS

Hirschowitz was inspired by the award-winning olive oil from Morgenster Estate to make this sauce for South Africa's kingklip fish. Kingklip is an eel-like, prehistoric-looking monster, which can weigh in at up to 60 pounds, with sweet, meaty flesh. Halibut lacks the kingklip's fierce appearance but has a similar taste.

 ¼ cup fresh lime juice
  1 tablespoon extra-virgin olive oil
Six 7-ounce skinless halibut fillets
  1 cup fish stock or bottled clam juice
 ½ cup dry white wine

  1 medium shallot, minced
  6 whole white peppercorns, plus freshly ground white pepper
  1 bay leaf
  1 cup heavy cream
Salt
 ½ cup green olives, such as Picholine, pitted and chopped
  2 tablespoons cold unsalted butter
  2 tablespoons chopped flat-leaf parsley

1. Preheat the oven to 450°. In a large, shallow dish, mix 2 tablespoons of the lime juice with the olive oil. Add the halibut fillets and turn to coat. Refrigerate for 15 minutes.

2. In a medium skillet, combine the fish stock, wine, shallot, white peppercorns, bay leaf and the remaining 2 tablespoons of lime juice. Boil over high heat until reduced to ½ cup, about 6 minutes. Add the cream, bring to a boil and simmer over moderately low heat until reduced to ⅔ cup, about 10 minutes. Strain the sauce into a small saucepan.

3. Season the halibut fillets with salt and white pepper and transfer them to a large rimmed baking sheet. Bake in the upper third of the oven until just cooked through, about 10 minutes.

A waitress at Africa Café; food at a *braai,* or barbecue; the staff at Le Quartier Français in Franschhoek.

4. Add the olives to the cream sauce and bring it to a boil. Pour in any accumulated fish juices. Remove the sauce from the heat and add the butter, whisking until incorporated. Stir in the parsley and season with salt and white pepper. Transfer the halibut fillets to a platter or warmed plates, spoon the sauce on top and serve.

WINE A racy South African Sauvignon Blanc will add another bright note to the tangy olive-lime butter.

Cape Malay Meat Loaf

8 SERVINGS

An enduring culinary legacy of colonial South Africa, this meat loaf with its custardy topping, called *bobotie* in Afrikaans, combines the twin Cape Malay loves for dried fruits and Eastern spices. It is traditionally served with yellow rice sweetened with honey. This version is from the Institute of Culinary Arts just outside Stellenbosch.

- 3 **slices of white bread, crusts removed and bread cut into 1-inch dice**
- 1½ **cups milk**
- 2 **tablespoons vegetable oil**
- 2 **large onions, finely chopped**
- 1 **large carrot, shredded**
- 1 **medium apple, peeled and shredded**
- 1½ **tablespoons curry powder**
- 2 **pounds ground lamb**
- ¼ **cup raisins**
- ¼ **cup mango chutney (see Note)**
- 1 **tablespoon apricot jam**
- 1 **tablespoon white wine vinegar**

Salt and freshly ground pepper
- 2 **large eggs**

1. Preheat the oven to 350°. Put the bread in a medium bowl, pour the milk over it and let stand until the bread is completely moistened, about 15 minutes.

2. In a large skillet, heat the vegetable oil. Add the onions and cook over high heat, stirring occasionally, for 2 minutes. Reduce the heat to moderately low and cook, stirring from time to time, until the onions are softened, about 10 minutes. Add the carrot and apple and cook over moderate heat for 3 minutes. Add the curry powder and cook, stirring, until fragrant, about 4 minutes. Add the lamb and cook, stirring to break up the meat, until no pink remains, about 5 minutes. Stir in the raisins, chutney, jam and vinegar and cook for 1 minute.

3. Squeeze the milk from the bread cubes and add the bread to the lamb mixture; reserve the milk. Using a fork, mash the softened bread into the lamb mixture until blended. Season with salt and pepper. Transfer the lamb mixture to a 9-by-13-inch baking dish and smooth the surface.

4. In a medium bowl, whisk the eggs with the reserved milk and pour the custard mixture evenly over the lamb. Bake the meat loaf for about 35 minutes, or until the custard is set on top. Let the meat loaf rest for 10 minutes before serving.

NOTE Toward the end of the 17th century, Dutch settlers imported Malay slaves who brought with them their Eastern spices (cardamom, ginger, garlic and so on), and dishes with clever spicing—chutneys, curries, *sosaties* (kebabs)—are among their most enduring culinary legacies.

MAKE AHEAD The recipe can be prepared through Step 3 and refrigerated overnight. Bring to room temperature before proceeding.

WINE A fruity Shiraz will play off the sweet notes in this dish. Or, opt for a uniquely South African Pinotage from Stellenbosch with deep mulberry flavors.

173

Photo Credits

Distributed by Sterling Publishing